FIVE ONE-ACT
FAITH PLAYS

Alan Avery

BLACKTHORN PRESS

Blackthorn Press, Blackthorn House
Middleton Rd, Pickering YO18 8AL
United Kingdom

www.blackthornpress.com

ISBN 9781906259273

Publication of this play does not imply availability for performance. Both
amateurs and professionals considering a production are *strongly* advised to apply
to the Blackthorn Press for written permission and quotation of a licensing fee
before starting rehearsals, advertising or booking a theatre.

Printed and bound by CPI Group (UK) Ltd, Croydon, CR0 4YY

CONTENTS

INTRODUCTION iv

STARDUST MELODY 1

NOW WE ARE SIXTY 17

THE WORD 49

GEORGE FOX AND MARGARET FELL
GET STUCK IN A LIFT 73

ONE OF THAT DESPISED PEOPLE 101

INTRODUCTION

These five one act plays were written over a seventeen year period from 1995 to 2012. They served two purposes. The first was to entertain the audiences and the second was to raise issues which could be discussed after the performance. Although a Quaker and a humanist myself, they were not written specifically for a Quaker audience and can be played before any group of people interested in being entertained and challenged at the same time.

Stardust Melody was written for pupils of Ackworth School where I was a teacher and was intended to get young people thinking about the afterlife and what makes for a good life while we are living.

The last four plays were written specifically for *The Quaker Theatre Company* and were toured throughout the UK, playing mostly in Friends Meeting Houses but also in village halls, church halls and even the crypt of Winchester Cathedral.

Now We Are Sixty deals with the problems of growing old and the strains that can take place within a marriage when faced with a growing apart, boredom and sexual problems. *The Word* is an adaptation of the five act play by Kaj Munk and examines what we mean by faith and belief. *George Fox and Margaret Fell Get Stuck in a Lift* asks how pacifist beliefs would hold up when faced with life and death problems which need hard decisions rather than theoretical musings. Finally, *One of That Despised People* tried to recreate the struggle of early Quakers to hang on to their faith under terrible provocation. The play has a futurist setting which allows a number of other issues to be brought into the light.

I would like to thank my fellow actors who contributed so much during rehearsals and on tour and the many contributors who made the staging of the plays possible. The plays are dedicated to my wife Anne, without whose support and enduring patience and love, none of them would have been written.

Alan Avery
Pickering 2012

STARDUST MELODY

A Play in One Act
by
Alan Avery

Characters:

MARY: A Girl of Fourteen to Sixteen
TRACY: A Girl of Fourteen to Sixteen
JACK: A Boy of 17 to 18

This play was first performed at Ackworth School, Pontefract in June 1995 with the following cast:

MARY: Christina Wunna
TRACY: Phoebe Craven
JACK: Richard Smith

STARDUST MELODY

MUSIC. Introductory music - "Stardust" by Nat King Cole.

MARY: *(Mary enters and falls centre stage, as if asleep. She is wearing a nightdress and dressing gown and slippers. She slowly wakes, sits up suddenly and then looks wonderingly around her)*

Hello! Hello, who's there? What is this? Look if it's money you want then my father will pay. This isn't funny you know. At least speak to me, tell me where I am. What time is it? Where is this place?

(She begins to explore the space looking for a door or anything to give her a clue as to where she is but finds nothing)

(screams) For God's sake say something! I'm here! Hello! Anybody out there I'm in here. I'm here, I'm here! Anybody - help.

(Again there is silence. Mary crumples to the floor and begins to cry. A light shines on a small table with a decanter and glass of water. Mary pours herself a glass)

Who are you? What do you want? I know my father will give you anything you want just let me out of here or speak to me. Anything but this.

(Mary crumples in one corner of the set. The door opens and the limp figure of Tracy staggers onto the set and collapses in the same place previously occupied by Mary. She is dressed as if for a dance)

TRACY: *(Goes through the same actions as Mary).*

What the bleeding hell is this? If this is your idea of a joke Darren Harkins you're dead meat. Now open the flaming door before I kick it down and your head with it! Come on, don't think you can scare me donkey brain. *(pause)* All right, if that's how you want to play it I'll just park meself here and wait till you get bored playing games and let me out. *(pause)* Either you let me out Harkins or I'm telling you, I'm straight round to the Coppers and then you're for it. Remand Home wasn't much fun I hear. My mum will knock you around something rotten when she gets to hear about this.

(She too wanders around the set looking for an opening and banging on the wall. As she comes to the place where Mary is she is just about to bang when Mary springs up and she is face to face with her. They stare at each other for a moment and then both speak at once)

2

MARY: Thank goodness. I thought I was going to be here forever. Look if you could just show me the way out I would be most grateful ...

TRACY: About time. You Harkin's bird? All right shows over. Take me back and we'll say no more about it ...

You ain't Harkin's bird are you?

MARY: Sorry?

TRACY: Darren Harkins - you ain't his bird. Nar - didn't think so. You're not his type. Too classy for Harkins, no ear-rings, nothing.

MARY: They're not allowed.

TRACY: What?

MARY: Ear-rings. We are not allowed to wear them. Only gold studs if we have our ears pierced - and I don't. Not yet anyway.

TRACY: You from the Convent?

MARY: That's right. How did you know?

TRACY: Don't get out much do you?

MARY: We get leave weekends and the holidays of course. But I don't usually go away for the weekends as my family aren't in England.

TRACY: Left you have they?

MARY: No, no. My father is in the diplomatic service so he's been sent to Italy this time - bit difficult just to pop over for the weekend.

TRACY: Yer, right. Look what's this all about? My mum will kill me if I don't take Wayne to school in the morning.

MARY: I don't know. Really, I don't. The last thing I remember was being ill in bed last night in the dorm - and then waking up here with a terrible head. And you?

TRACY: Down at Toffs till late last night - dancing. I was just crossing the road on the way to the bus when I suppose I was jumped. They must have put a blanket over me head - doped me I suppose. Then like you here I am. Where's the way out?

MARY: I couldn't find one.

TRACY: Me neither. Anything to eat or drink?

MARY: I got a glass of water from there.

(Tracy goes over to the table and pours herself a drink)

TRACY: You there whoever you are? I could do with a rum and coke. Can you hear me? You must have made a mistake about me. You'll get something for her ladyship there but no one is going to pay up for me. It'll take 'em a week before they even realise I'm missing. Who the hell did you think I was - Madonna slumming it?

MARY: You think we've been kidnapped. That's what I thought as well. I'm sure my father will pay for both of us once he finds out. Couldn't your father put any money together?

TRACY: Don't make me laugh. We haven't even seen the old man since Wayne was born. That was six years ago.

MARY: Then why have they taken you?

TRACY: Search me. Like I said, they must have made a mistake. *(aloud)* Listen bone heads, once you find out I ain't who you think I am you can just let me go - I wont say nuffink about her - you can trust me.

MARY: Thanks.

TRACY: That's O.K. Got to look after number one haven't you. *(whispers)* Look, if I can get out I'd make sure they knew about you - O.K.

MARY: Yes, O.K. Sorry. They're bound to be looking for me now. What time is it?

TRACY: It's - Hey, my watch has gone!

MARY: Mine too. I suppose they took them to disorientate us.

4

TRACY: No-one's disontating me. Anyone who comes near me gets it. You listening?

MARY: Imagine Miss Evans face when she finds me gone.

TRACY: Whose Miss Evans?

MARY: My Housemistress.

TRACY: Cleaning lady like. Mum does that down the local Job Centre.

MARY: Job Centre?

TRACY: Dole office.

MARY: She's not a cleaning lady. She looks after us - like a mum.

TRACY: Ain't you got a mum then?

MARY: Yes, of course, I told you ...

TRACY: Oh yeh, in Italy.

MARY: They're bound to be looking everywhere for me. They might think I've run away. Once they can't find me they are sure to phone the police.

TRACY: Police. I don't want nuffink to do with the police. Leave me out of it.

MARY: But the police will find us and arrest these people and set us free.

TRACY: Just leave me out of the police.

MARY: Have you done something wrong?

TRACY: What's it got to do with you Miss la -de - da.

MARY: Sorry, I was only concerned.

TRACY: Yer, well just mind your own business and concentrate on getting us out of here.

MARY: How old are you?

TRACY: Fourteen, if it's any of your business.

MARY: Me too. Funny, I thought you were older.

TRACY: That right. Well, it ain't the years but the mileage as me old Dad used to say.

MARY: You still remember him then?

TRACY: Course I do. You don't forget your own Dad.

MARY: But your father must have left when you were seven. Can you really remember what he said after all these years?

TRACY: Course I can. Funny though, I never said that before - about the mileage - but I'm sure he used to say it. Unless I heard it somewhere else, on the telly like.

MARY: You have a T.V. in your own home?

TRACY: Sure I have. Everyone has.

MARY: We've just got one at school - for the schools' programmes but Miss Evans sometimes lets us watch the children's programmes. I like that new one, Dr Who, but it's really scary. Some of the younger ones hide behind the sofa.

TRACY: Dr Who? Never heard of him. Must be on BBC 2 or something. I just watch "TFI Friday" or porn videos when me mum's out.

MARY: Videos?

TRACY: Videos. You know, Videos. Stone me what sort of place is that Convent?

MARY: It's very nice thank you but we haven't got any videos to use.

TRACY: "It's very nice thank you". You lot make me ill.

MARY: What do you mean, "you lot"?

TRACY: You lot down the Convent with your fancy uniforms and posh accents, playing tennis and hockey and going to all those nice places in your holidays. Don't know you're born.

6

MARY: Don't you like your school then? Is it a Grammar School or one of the Secondary Moderns?

TRACY: Hey? Don't know about that. It's just the local comp where all the kids around here go.

MARY: Comp?

TRACY: Yer, comp - Comprehensive. You know.

MARY: It's not a term I've heard before. Did you have to pass your eleven plus to go there?

TRACY: Forget it will you. We aint on the same planet. Got a boy friend?

MARY: Of course not. I'm far too young. Anyway, we don't get to see many boys at the Convent. Just once a year when the boys from St Joseph's come over for the Christmas dance.

TRACY: Don't you fancy any of the boys at your school then?

MARY: I've told you we only get to mix with boys ...

TRACY: Don't give me that. I know loads of boys from the Convent. My mate Judy went out with Tom Haycock for ages before he packed her in. You must know Tom Haycock!

MARY: No. He must be at St Joseph's.

TRACY: You trying to be funny or sumink. St Joseph's closed years ago. They joined up with your place to make a go of it.

MARY: No, no you must be thinking of some other schools.

TRACY: Forget it. You must have had a bang on the head if you ask me. Sent you right round the twist.

MARY: Have you - got a boy friend?

TRACY: Yer, course I have. Well sort of.

MARY: How can you sort of have a boy friend?

TRACY: I knock around with Darren Harkins a bit when he asks me but he's no good. Always in trouble, always two timing me.

MARY: Two timing?

TRACY: Seeing other girls when he tells me he's busy - that sort of thing. Well if he can play the field, so can I. John King always fancied me. I'll give him the works see if I can get him to take me out.

MARY: Do they - kiss you - these boys?

TRACY: What do you think? Mind you I never let it go any further. Well not much further any way.

MARY: I should say not!

TRACY: Can't be too careful these days. Me mum's always trying to get me on the pill but I don't fancy it.

MARY: The pill. I am sorry, I didn't know you were ill. Is it serious?

TRACY: Are you taking the mick or what?

MARY: Sorry?

TRACY: Never mind.   You really are a goody-goody aren't you?

MARY: I'm no different from any of the other girls.

TRACY: Different from any other girl I've ever met.

MARY: Are you hungry?

TRACY: I wouldn't say no to a big Mac?

MARY: Is he one of your boy friends?

TRACY: You are taking the mick. I'll push your face in you smart-arsed cow.

(Tracy attacks Mary kneeling on her shoulders and slapping her face. The door opens and Jack stumbles in collapsing in the centre of the stage. He wears a silver or white boiler suit)

TRACY: Here, he's not bad looking is he. Wonder who he is?

MARY: Are you all right? I say, can you hear me? Get me some water will you.

TRACY: Get it yourself. I ain't your servant.

MARY: *(fetches a glass of water)* What are you doing?

TRACY: Going through his pockets - see if we can find out anything about him.

MARY: Do you think we should. He might get angry.

TRACY: I can handle him. Hello what's this? *(Tracy finds a small metallic object in Jack's pocket)* I aint never seen anything like this before. Must be some kind of lighter.

MARY: He doesn't look like the kind of boy who would smoke.

JACK: Oh my head. Who are you?

TRACY: We were here first. You tell us who you are and then we might tell you who we are.

JACK: Jack Symonds.

MARY: What happened to you Jack?

JACK: The shuttle was making its approach O.K. We were all undoing our servobelts when there was a lurch to port and a loud bang, a flash. I remember being thrown up in the air. Then I woke up here. Where is this place?

TRACY: Search us. What's this?

JACK: My communicator. Give it here. Hello this is DF457, Jack Symonds. Come in. Respond. Funny it seems to be dead. These things never break down. 100% through every time, first time. That's what the Company said.

MARY: We think we have been kidnapped. At least I have - Tracy thinks she was a mistake. Would anyone want to kidnap you? Are your parents rich?

JACK: You haven't told me who you are. Your friend is Tracy, I have heard that but who are you?

MARY: Mary. Mary Knowles. I am at the Convent but I think I have been kidnapped because my family is rich.

JACK: And you Tracy, what about you?

TRACY: Like she said, just a mistake if you ask me. We aint got no money so what these people are playing at I don't know.

JACK: What people?

TRACY: Whoever nabbed us?

JACK: Nabbed?

TRACY: Now don't you start. Whoever kidnapped us if you like.

JACK: But why would anyone resort to kidnapping these days? What would be the benefit for them?

TRACY: Money dumbo - why else?

JACK: But money has been redundant for years - you know that - they must know that. What can they hope to gain. My social group has no influence with the World Council. I am of no individual importance.

TRACY: Let me ask you a question Jack. Who is the Prime Minister?

JACK: Of where?

TRACY: England of course, where else!

MARY: She means the United Kingdom actually.

TRACY: Shut up, actually. Well?

JACK: The leader of the British Regional Council? I suppose it must still be Robinson but who cares about local government these days? It's whoever gets the job at the World Council that matters. Heslop is the woman there at the moment.

TRACY: Mary - who is Prime Minister? Come on.

MARY: Harold Wilson of course, everyone knows that ... don't they?

TRACY: *(names the current Prime Minister. Tony Blaire when this play was written)*

MARY: What?

TRACY: Tony Blaire. It's Tony Blaire. Tony Blaire is the Prime Minister - right!

JACK: We were doing about him in history the other day. Amazing he could get away with it for all those years.

TRACY: Top twenty. Whose top this week Jack?

JACK: That group from the Pacific Region, the one that uses pulsar-vobes. You know it's the theme tune for World News.

MARY: It's the Beatles. Even I know that.

TRACY: *(names a currently popular group.)*

MARY: What's going on? I don't understand.

JACK: We seem to have widely diverse cultural backgrounds.

TRACY: We're dead.

MARY: What?

JACK: Speak for yourself. I feel fine.

TRACY: Don't you see. She was ill in bed before she came here, I was crossing the road, you were in some kind of aeroplane accident. We none of us made it. We all died and now we are here. Wherever this is.

MARY: Hell. Surely not heaven. Limbo?

JACK: What's that?

MARY: A sort of in-between world. Between heaven and hell where souls go before they can be accepted into heaven.

JACK: You are talking about religion aren't you. We still pick up bits of it even though it's banned.

TRACY: How can you ban religion?

JACK: The World Council did. It was causing so many wars it had to be eradicated like the flu and flags. Look, we can soon clear this up. Mary, when were you born?

MARY: 1952.

JACK: Tracy?

TRACY: 1984. You?

JACK: 2020.

MARY: It's true we are dead. But why this? Why three people from different times thrown together like this?

JACK: If there is life after death - and this is it - it's supposed to be forever isn't it? Infinity?

TRACY: Yeh, me dad used to say "enjoy yourself while you can - you're a long time dead."

JACK: Quite. So the years that separate us are meaningless when compared to infinity. If time has any meaning.

TRACY: This is all too deep for me. Look you Mary, you're the religious one. How do we get out of here? How do we get back?

MARY: It's all got to do with purgatory. That's it, this must be purgatory. "Before the soul of a person who has died can enjoy union with God it may have to experience purgatory, that is to say, a state or place where it is purified of its sins and these souls in purgatory can be helped by the prayers of the people on Earth. If you reject the will of God you remain in hell, that is separated from God, for ever."

TRACY: You mean the only way out of here is if the people back home pray for us?

MARY: Yes, I think so.

TRACY: Well that leaves me out. My lot haven't been to church since Nan died. I doubt they even know how to pray.

JACK: Prayer is banned along with religion. My family will mourn for me privately at home. No public prayers. But you should be all right Mary. Your circle of associates will surely pray for you. What are you doing here anyway?

TRACY: Yeh, that's right. Why aint you gone straight to heaven? What you ever had the chance to do wrong? Didn't you do your homework or something?

MARY: I must have had impure thoughts. I don't think I have actually committed any mortal sins. What about you Tracy, Jack?

JACK: We have all done things we regret.

TRACY: Too right. It was me drove me dad away. Broke me mum up.

MARY: Surely not. How could a young girl ...

TRACY: Shut up will you! What do you know about anything?

MARY: Sorry. I didn't mean ...

JACK: May as well get it off your chest Tracy. We could be here for ever. Clear your conscience while you can.

TRACY: I aint never said this to anyone else before ... it's hard to say it out loud.

MARY: We can only listen, Tracy, and try and understand.

TRACY: O.K.   I don't want no daft comments.

JACK: Of course not.

TRACY: I saw me dad coming out of a pub with this woman all over him. I got so ... angry ... at him, not her. I ran home to me mum and told her. Don't ask me why, I never really cared for me mum, it was always me Dad.

MARY: What happened?

TRACY: When me Dad got home there was one hell of a row. I didn't mind that - you got used to it. It was the look in me Dad's eyes when he found out it was me who shopped him. He looked at me really hurt as if it was me that had let him down. He left or got slung out by me mum. I aint seen him since.

MARY: But you were only a little girl. You could have no idea of the consequences of telling your mother.

JACK: The real fault lay with your father for being unfaithful. If he had remained constant to your mother none of it would have happened. You can't blame yourself. Someone else would have told her eventually.

TRACY: Yeh, I've told meself all that. It was just the look in his eyes. I can't ever forget it. I just wanted to see me Dad again and tell him I was sorry. Now I don't suppose I ever will. Thanks for listening you two. No-one ever listened before. I somehow feel better now - sort of lighter.

JACK: Do you think your parents will get together again when they hear about - your death? Could that be what this is all about?

TRACY: Nah. Me mum's got this boyfriend been living with us for years. He's all right I suppose. Don't know if me dad is even alive.

JACK: What would you say to him if you could?

TRACY: What could I say? Sorry. That I ... loved him and just want to see him again. To hear his laugh one more time.

(A man's voice is heard off stage, coming as if from a distance. "Tracy look out! My God, is she dead?" *Another voice.* "No the car just clipped her. I think she's coming round." *Man's voice.* Tracy, it's me, your Dad. They said I'd find you here. Can you hear me?")

TRACY: I have to go. It's me Dad. Goodbye you two. Thanks. *(exit)*

MARY: I don't understand. Why has she gone? Why are we still here?

JACK: She seems to have said what was hidden inside her. She talked to us, said what she had always wanted to say and returned for another chance to make a life for herself.

MARY: Do you think that she will be happy with her father? What about her mother?

JACK: Hard to say but somehow I think Tracy will be happier. Just because her mother and father don't love each other it doesn't mean she can't love them both.

MARY: I suppose you're right. Where does that leave us?

JACK: Right here with nowhere to go and only each other to talk to. Tracy said something that still puzzles me.

MARY: What's that?

JACK: You. Why are you here? If you died, why not straight to heaven - if there is such a place. What could you possibly have done wrong?

MARY: I don't know. I don't want to talk about it.

JACK: Then there is something. Well tell me if you want to. I seem to have plenty of time.

MARY: I ... No. If I tell you Jack, will you promise ...

JACK: Not to tell anyone else? I don't see many people to tell, do you?

MARY: No. Of course not. But you wont think any the worse of me. I like you Jack. I don't want you to think badly of me.

JACK: Mary, you are a sweet innocent girl. How could anyone not like you.

MARY: I have done a terrible thing. *(She begins to cry. Jack takes her in his arms to comfort her.)*

JACK: All right Mary, I'm listening.

MARY: It was last year. We had a new girl at the Convent. A day girl. She really got on my nerves. Always going on about her boyfriends and how she did this and did that and what a lot of fuddy-duddies we all were at the Convent - not like at her old school.

JACK: Well?

MARY: Well, I got the other girls to gang up on her. You know, stop talking whenever she came into the room. No-one would sit next to her or talk to her at break.

JACK: That was unkind of you.

MARY: I know that now. But the worse thing was that in the end she tried to ..to kill herself. She didn't - her parents found her in time. Then it all came out. She didn't have any boyfriends at all. She never even went out in the evening just sat in her room moping. All the boys and the parties were just fantasies. She just wanted to appear big in front of us.

15

JACK: I see. What happened?

MARY: Oh, her parents took her away. But don't you see she could have killed herself and it would have been my fault. I could have been kind and helped her but I was cruel and almost destroyed her.

JACK: Then you think that's why you're here?

MARY: Yes, I think so.

JACK: Why do you think you turned against her like that? It doesn't seem in your nature.

MARY: It was all the talk about boys. It made me so, so. I don't know. Kiss me Jack.

JACK: What?

MARY: Kiss me. I've never been kissed by a boy in all my life and now I never will be. Don't you understand?

JACK: Yes, of course. *(He gently kisses her)*

MARY: Thank you. *(She kisses him.)* You must think me very forward. I'm not at all.

JACK: I think you're the most wonderful girl I've ever met.

MARY: Do you mean that? Do you mean that? Are all boys like you?

JACK: That's for you to find out Mary. Have a wonderful life.

MRS EVANS *(Voice off)* Is she going to be all right Doctor?

DOCTOR: *(Voice off)* It was touch and go there for a while Miss Evans but I think she will be all right now.

MARY: Jack. I have to go. I'll never forget you. *(exit)*

JACK: Yes you will Mary. And Tracy. And all this. In the end, all we have is each other and the power to love and forgive. So tired. Must sleep. *(He curls up and sleeps centre stage. Music plays softly. He suddenly wakes up with a start)* Hello! Hello, who's there? What is this? Look if it's money you want then my father will pay. This isn't funny you know. At least speak to me, tell me where I am. What time is it? Where is this place?

END

16

NOW WE ARE SIXTY

A Play in One Act
by
Alan Avery

Characters:

SIMON: A Man aged sixty
MEGAN: A Woman, aged fifty to sixty, his wife
MARALYN: A young woman

This play was first performed at Pickering Quaker Meeting House on 3rd October 2009 with the following cast:

SIMON: Alan Avery
MEGAN: Judy Emmet
MARALYN: Katy Moore

NOW WE ARE SIXTY

On speaker: *'Approach old age with courage and hope. As far as possible, make arrangements for your care in good time, so that an undue burden does not fall on others. Although old age may bring increasing disability and loneliness, it can also bring serenity, detachment and wisdom. Pray that in your final years you may be enabled to find new ways of receiving and reflecting God's love.'*

A tub chair. A carpet. A lamp back stage, lit, draped with bunting. Two empty bottles of wine on the floor. A large box. A book shelf. A Photo. A CD Player with CDs. MUSIC: 'Hound Dog'. Enter Simon, dressed as Elvis Presley. He surveys the audience and then sits in chair SR and, head back snores loudly as lights come up. Fade music. Enter Megan in dressing gown with mug of tea. She holds Simon's nose until he wakes up.

MEGAN: Tea.

SIMON: Well, thankyouveramuch.

MEGAN: You can stop it now. I didn't move you. Couldn't move you. So I left you. *(Megan turns out the light and taking the two bottles exits)*

SIMON: Mm.

MEGAN: *(Off stage)* I think it all went very well.

SIMON: Yes.

MEGAN: I didn't even recognise half the people. I assume they've all gone. I just went to bed and left you to it. Who were they?

SIMON: Must have been partners of people from the lab – where I worked – must get used to using the past tense now. And weren't there some of your friends from the bank?

MEGAN: Colleagues.

SIMON: Oh.

MEGAN: You seemed to be enjoying yourself anyway. You and Sandra Norbrey.

SIMON: Who?

18

MEGAN: *(Enters with own tea)* Sandra Norbrey. She came as Cleopatra. She wore that jade pendant. Just about all she was wearing. At our age. Ridiculous.

SIMON: I don't know. I mean she has looked after herself. She looked fine. Didn't John make an incredible Mrs Thatcher?

MEGAN: Amazing. Did you notice he had no trouble with the high heels?

SIMON: What?

MEGAN: I mean, put most blokes in a pair of high heals and they are all over the place but he was even dancing in them.

SIMON: Oh yes … You don't think…? No, not John.

MEGAN: Well ….Are you going to Meeting this morning?

SIMON: Yes. I thought I would keep the costume on, it doesn't have to be back until tomorrow, arrive a minute late, swerve past Jack on the door and make an entrance. Sit somewhere different to cause confusion and then ten minutes in, stand and do a medley of Elvis's greatest hits *(He sings)* 'I just want to be/Your Teddy Bear/ Put a chain around my neck/And lead me anywhere/Just want to be your Teddy Bear. Thankyouverramuch. What do you think?

MEGAN: Yes, I can see Doris getting into the spirit of the occasion – 'There is a table top sale at the Methodists this Saturday and Elvis has left the building'. Go for it. But don't you think there might be objections?

SIMON: Nowhere is it written 'thou shalt not attend Meeting dressed as Elvis Presley'.

MEGAN: I meant the singing.

SIMON: Friends do sing. It's not nice, but they do.

MEGAN: I meant *you* singing.

SIMON: Are you implying I can't sing?

MEGAN: Would I? You must be the only person left in the region who can even remember Elvis Presley.

SIMON: I'm not going anyway. Heart's prepared. Mind's out of it.

MEGAN: Good, you can help me tidy up and then there is all that stuff to go to the tip. And can you please do something about that bloody box your friends from the lab dragged in. I've been falling over it all morning. What is it anyway? Looks like a grandfather clock. A high-tech one no doubt that no-one will want to buy, like all the other junk you produce – produced.

SIMON: On the other hand, perhaps it would do me good to get an hour's peace and quiet.

MEGAN: *(Looking in mirror on fourth wall)* I haven't let myself go. Not too much. Have I?

SIMON: Who said you had?

MEGAN: You did.

SIMON: Never! When did I say that?

MEGAN: You said that Sandra Norbrey hadn't let herself go, implying that I had.

SIMON: Feminine logic! If I say something nice about one woman it does not imply I am criticising all other women or one other woman in particular i.e. you. If I had criticised Sandra what's-her-name for being inappropriately dressed for a sixtieth birthday – which she wasn't by the way, I thought it was jolly sporting of her – does that mean I am praising all other women for wearing the 'correct' boring outfits?

MEGAN: So I was boring. Tony Smedley said I looked very nice as Queen Victoria.

SIMON: I thought you were supposed to be Dame Madonna?

MEGAN: I was.

SIMON: Well, you did look nice.

MEGAN: Boring but nice.

SIMON: I am not going to be drawn into an argument I can't win.

MEGAN: Were we arguing? I thought we were discussing Sandra Norbrey.

SIMON: You were discussing her. I remain neutral.

MEGAN: Do take that ridiculous costume off. I jump every time I see you in it.

SIMON: All right. Let me at least drink my tea.

MEGAN: I don't know why you still go to Meeting anyway. You don't believe a word of it.

SIMON: Some of it.

MEGAN: What?

SIMON: Enough.

MEGAN: You sit there in your stony silence, not even knowing what the person sitting next to you believes, and even when anybody speaks, it's all personal stuff which you could talk about over a cup of tea at home. The only time I asked what Quakers believed, the answer I got was that he had to catch a bus and read this big red book. It's all form with no substance.

SIMON: Meeting for worship is …

MEGAN: Worshiping what? I've heard everything from God in majesty in Heaven to the divine spirit that rules the universe to the power of the trees and flowers. Why not admit you are a Sunday morning tea party with pretensions.

SIMON: Well, Friends are all different with different ideas.

MEGAN: Then you might as well go into any church in town, those that are left or haven't become social centres or been burned down. Why hasn't anybody burned the Meeting House down or at least smashed the windows?

SIMON: I don't think people know we exist or if they do, they think we are pretty harmless. We seem to have avoided most of the scandals and the bricks.

MEGAN: Mm. Well you be careful if you do go. Anyone walking the streets on a Sunday morning seems to be fair game these days. At least you don't have to put on a Sunday best but do take the costume off.

SIMON: I will.

MEGAN: I'm going for a shower.

SIMON: Call me when you need your back doing.

MEGAN: I can do my own back. Costume. Glasses need putting away. Stuff for the tip and that bloody crate. *(Exit Megan)*

SIMON: Yes my love. *(Takes off costume while examining the crate)* What have those jokers been up to now? As long as it doesn't explode when I open it. *(He prises off the lid)* Bloody Nora. *(Simon takes out a manual, a remote control and a small bottle of oil. He points the control into the box but nothing happens. He breathes on the control and tries again. Maralyn's upper torso appears, apparently naked. She does not look at Simon but puts a piece of bubble wrap in her mouth, spits it out and then examines the box)*

SIMON: Hello.

(Maralyn turns to the sound of Simon's voice but is then distracted by the site of her own hand which she examines. She then begins to examine her feet)

SIMON: Can you hear me?

(Maralyn again looks at Simon and slowly examines him from head to foot)

MARALYN: Mm.

SIMON: Aha! My name is Simon. What is …?

MARALYN: Ich heisse, ich heisse …

SIMON: Wait, wait, language, language, Arabic, Danish , English.

MARALYN: My name is …, my name is …enter name. My name is …, my name is… enter name.

SIMON: Yes, yes. *(He looks at the manual)* Maralyn. I'm going to call you Maralyn.

MARALYN: My name is Maralyn. What is your name?

SIMON: Simon. Simon.

MARALYN: Hello, Simon. Simon.

SIMON: No, no, just Simon.

MARALYN: Hello, No, no just Simon

SIMON: Aghhh. *(Plays with control)*

MARALYN: My name is Maralyn. What is your name?

SIMON: Simon.

MARALYN: Hello, Simon.

SIMON: Hello Maralyn. Can I help you out? *(He holds out his hands, which Maralyn takes. She rises from the box, slowly finding her feet. She stumbles and Simon helps her to her feet. She takes a few faltering steps helped by Simon)* Good, good, you are getting the hang of it. You look cold. Put this on. *(He takes the Elvis costume from the chair and offers it to Maralyn who looks at it but does not know what to do. Simon dresses her in the costume)* Say, 'thank you'.

MARALYN: Thank you. Thank you Simon.

SIMON: *(Again, consulting the manual)* Look, I have to top up your fluids. So turn around. *(She does not move. He turns goes behind her)* Ah, here. *(He fills up Maralyn's fluids with the oil bottle)* Feel better?

MARALYN: Yes. Thank you Simon. It feels better. *(She begins to move her arms and to walk and speak more naturally. Simon is flicking through the manual)*

SIMON: Yes, It makes you look a lot better. Now, I am going to read you something and you have to copy what I am saying. Do you understand? Never mind, sit next to me and listen. *(Simon sits. Maralyn kneels at Simon's feet and sucks her thumb)* 'The Mole had been working very hard all the morning, spring-cleaning his little home.' Now you. You say it. 'The Mole had been working..'.

MARALYN: 'The Mole had been working'.

SIMON: '..very hard all the morning'.

MARALYN: 'Very hard all the morning'.

SIMON: '..spring-cleaning his little home.'

MARALYN: 'Spring-cleaning his little home.'

SIMON: 'First with brooms, then with dusters...'

MARALYN: 'First with brooms, then with dusters…'

SIMON: Well, you got the hang of that quickly enough. Let's try this one. 'It is a truth universally acknowledged, that a single man in possession of a good fortune, must be in want of a wife.'

MARALYN: 'It is a truth universally acknowledged, that a single man in possession of a good fortune, must be in want of a wife. However little known the feelings or views of such a man' (I have this one) 'may be on first entering a neighbourhood …'

SIMON: That's fine, good, stop. Look, I have to get dressed, so I'll just switch you off…

MARALYN: You can't.

SIMON: What?

MARALYN: I am here with you now, so there is no going back.

SIMON: Well, that's new. All right. But don't leave this room and no noise. I'll be back in a moment. Stay out of trouble. *(Exit Simon)*

MARALYN: Goodbye Simon. See you soon. *(Maralyn begins to look around her. She finds a magazine and begins to copy some of the poses of the models in it. She finds a CD player and switches it on. Elvis Presley 'Heartbreak Hotel' very loud. Off stage* MEGAN: Turn that bloody racket off. You must be the only man left who still listens to Elvis Presley. *Maralyn turns off CD takes out the CD and scans it with her finger. She picks up a photo. She tries to see herself in the glass. She then notices mirror on fourth wall and examines her face and body. Enter Megan looking for her glasses which she finds on the shelves. Maralyn has her back to her)*

MEGAN: I'm just popping round to the hypermart. We seem to be out of everything after last night. Do you want anything? I wont be long. Do take that bloody costume off. *Exit Megan*

MARALYN: Hello, my name is …..Oh!

SIMON: *(Enter Simon dressed)* Everything O.K.?

MARALYN: Fine thank you Simon. Who was that shouting?

SIMON: Oh, Megan my wife. You can say hello in a minute when she comes down. You will be a surprise.

MARALYN: I think I just met her. She went out. I don't think she saw me. Did you want anything?

SIMON: In general or specifically just now?

MARALYN: Who is Elvis Presley? Can I meet him? I need my own long mirror. I would like a dress. None of the others wear these things. Why can't I have a dress like all the others?

SIMON: Others? What others? Have you been outside? I told you to stay in this room.

MARALYN: It's not fair. I bet all the other Simons get nice dresses and underwear for their Maralyns but I have to go around in this old thing. I bet I look awful. I need a long mirror to see what I look like.

SIMON: Who have you been speaking to?

MARALYN: No one would want to speak to me the way I look…

SIMON: Who?

MARALYN: In the magazine.

SIMON: Ah, that. I can explain about that. You see …

MARALYN: It's not as if I ask for much, is it? Just a few dresses and some makeup and a mirror to see myself and a comb and a television and a computer. I bet all the other Marlayns get those things without even having to ask, while I have to go around looking like this. Aren't you ashamed of me? I could look really nice for you if you would only …

SIMON: Yes, all right, all right. I'll find you some things later.

MARALYN: When?

SIMON: Later. I said later.

MARALYN: Today? Later today?

25

SIMON: Yes, today. I'm sure we can find some old things of Megan's that will fit you.

MARALYN: I can't wear those. They will be ancient. All the other Maralyns will laugh at me. Can't I have some new things?

SIMON: Megan's things will have to do around the house. You can have something new once the clothes shops open tomorrow. Or whenever you are ready to leave the house.

MARALYN: Oh! *(Clutches her stomach in pain)* What..?

SIMON: Are you all right – where's that bloody manual?

MARALYN: It's all right. I'm all right. Simon?

SIMON: Yes.

MARALYN: Do you think I am attractively built?

SIMON: Very. They put you together well.

MARALYN: Can I touch you?

SIMON: Yes, I don't see why not.

MARALYN: *(She feels Simon's face)* You can kiss me. Please kiss me. I have never been kissed. *(Simon pecks her on the forehead. Maralyn takes hold of Simon's head and kisses him)*

SIMON: Now look Maralyn ...

MARALYN: You can fuck me if you want. Here on the carpet.

SIMON: Bloody hell. Listen Maralyn, that's very kind, very generous of you and I am extremely flattered, but it doesn't work like that.

MARALYN: Not on the carpet?

SIMON: No, not on the carpet or the kitchen table or in the bedroom.

MARALYN: Where then?

SIMON: Nowhere. People – women – just don't behave like that. Things like that take a little more time, a little more thought.

MARALYN: I am thinking about it. I can't seem to think of anything else at the moment.

SIMON: Try and think of something – anything – do you like music. What's on the tainmentcentre?

MARALYN: I have scanned it. *(Music begins. Maralyn Sings)*

Can't you see
I love you
Please don't break my heart in two
That's not hard to do
'Cause I don't have a wooden heart
And if you say goodbye
Then I know that I would cry
Maybe I would die
'Cause I don't have a wooden heart
There's no strings upon this love of mine
It was always you from the start
Treat me nice
Treat me good
Treat me like you really should
'Cause I'm not made of wood
And I don't have a wooden heart

Muss i denn, muss i denn
Zum Stadtele hinaus
Stadtele hinaus
Und du, mein schatz, bleibst hier? [repeat this verse]

There's no strings upon this love of mine
It was always you from the start
Sei mir gut
Sei mir gut
Sei mir wie du wirklich sollst
Wie du wirklich sollst
'Cause I don't have a wooden heart.

SIMON: That was great. The king would have been proud of you. *(He kisses Maralyn. They begin to move onto the carpet)*

27

MEGAN: *(Off stage)* Surprisingly few people in the shops for a Sunday.

SIMON: Sod it. Sod it… *(Exit Simon)*

MEGAN: *(Enters)* Nothing much on the shelves of course. I didn't get you any peanuts, I don't want you getting fat again.

MARALYN: Hello.

MEGAN: Oh! Hello. I thought you were Simon. The costume…

MARALYN: No. My name is Maralyn. Simon gave me the costume, as I had no clothes.

MEGAN: Ah … yes. I don't seem to remember you from last night did you come on your own?

MARALYN: Yes, I think so.

MEGAN: It sounds as though you had a good time. Do you have far to go? Are you local?

MARALYN: Yes.

MEGAN: I can't place your face. Who is your mother? Do I know her?

MARALYN: *(Maralyn looks at the crate)* I don't think …..

MEGAN: Sorry, I'm being nosy. Can I ring for a taxi for you? Would you like a drink while you are waiting?

MARALYN: No thank you. Simon topped me up before you came back.

MEGAN: Did he indeed. I meant a coffee.

MARALYN: No thank you. I am not allowed.

MEGAN: Oh, it's not as bad for your heart as they say. Some water then?

MARALYN: No, that would be the end of me.

MEGAN: Well, the ultimate diet. You really don't need to worry about that, not for a few more years.

MARALYN: Simon said you might have some clothes I could have …

MEGAN: Until yours turn up. Yes, well I might have something loose at the back of the wardrobe you could get into.

MARALYN: I expect Elvis would like his costume back.

MEGAN: Yes, …quite.

MARALYN: Do you have anything in blue? Blue is my colour.

MEGAN: Possibly. Come up to the bedroom and see what there is. Then we can get you that taxi. Where is Simon?

MARALYN: He left very quickly and went upstairs.

MEGAN: Last night catching up on him. He always overdoes it.

MARALYN: No, I think it might have been me.

MEGAN: Sorry?

MARALYN: He was just about to fuck me, here on the carpet but then you came home.

MEGAN: What?

MARALYN: He didn't want to at first but I sang for him and then he really wanted to.

MEGAN: Oh, I see. You are pulling my leg.

MARALYN: No.

MEGAN: What did you sing?

MARALYN: A song I found on this disc.

MEGAN: *(Looking at the disc)* Yes, I see. Look, keep the damn costume and just go will you.

MARALYN: I can't. Simon said I had to stay here.

MEGAN: Never mind what Simon said, just be on your way.

MARALYN: Don't you sing for Simon?

MEGAN: No, I bloody well don't.

MARALYN: Does he kiss you like he kissed me?

MEGAN: That is none of your business young lady. Look, I am not sure what has been going on here and I really don't want to know so just keep the costume and see yourself out. The front door is there.

MARALYN: *(Picking up picture)* Who are the small people?

MEGAN: The children.

MARALYN: Yes, the children. Are they yours?

MEGAN: Look, I don't want....

MARALYN: They look like you.

MEGAN: They are my sister's children, if you must know.

MARALYN: You have no children?

MEGAN: No. Now if you would just...

MARALYN: You didn't function correctly?

MEGAN: No, as you so charmingly put it, I didn't function correctly.

MARALYN: Could you not be repaired?

MEGAN: I really do not want to discuss ...

MARALYN: I suppose it is too late now for you to be repaired. You must be obsolete. It would hardly be worth the trouble.

MEGAN: Are you laughing at me because if you are ....

SIMON: *(Entering)* Ah, I see you two have met.

MEGAN: Yes, Maralyn, or whatever her name is ...

MARALYN: My name is Maralyn.

MEGAN: Shut up!

MARALYN: It is.

MEGAN: Has been telling me what you two were up to while I was out. Well?

SIMON: Well?

MEGAN: Is it true?

SIMON: What has she been saying?

MEGAN: That you got her drunk, listened to some sentimental twaddle she sang you and then were just about to, to ... here on the carpet, my carpet.

SIMON: Our carpet.

MEGAN: Never mind whose carpet it is ...is it true?

SIMON: Yes, but ...

MEGAN: *(Sits deflated on the chair)* Well at least you are honest. But you didn't...

SIMON: No.

MARALYN: You came home and then Simon didn't want to any more.

SIMON: Please be quiet Maralyn.

MARALYN: Yes Simon.

MEGAN: Yes Simon. You've got her well trained, very submissive. Was that part of the attraction?

SIMON: You really don't understand.

MEGAN: I think I understand very well, thank you. Now what?

SIMON: What?

MEGAN: You are acting as if this is quite normal, as if nothing has happened.

SIMON: But nothing did happen.

MEGAN: If I had stopped to talk to Mrs Pattel or taken the biscuits back to the shelf, then it would have, wouldn't it? I would have come in to find you two … here …

SIMON: Yes, but . . .

MEGAN: So don't pretend that nothing happened. *(To Maralyn)* Look will you just get out and leave us alone. Haven't you done enough damage?

MARALYN: Simon?

SIMON: I really think you are over-reacting. I was wrong to get involved with Maralyn in that way. I admit it. I am sorry.

MEGAN: Oh, well that's all right then. How would you have felt if you had come home and found me and Tony Smedley hard at it in the middle of the living room?

MARALYN: Who is Tony Smedley?

SIMON: Shush! Angry of course. Look, I said I am sorry. Nothing really happened. Let's just let things go on as before.

MEGAN: No. They can't. I don't know who this girl is and quite frankly she doesn't seem the sharpest knife in the drawer, especially if she finds you overwhelmingly desirable, but she might have done us both a favour.

SIMON: What?

MEGAN: It needed something like this to bring it all out into the open, clear the air.

SIMON: Bring all what out?

MEGAN: Us, us you fool. Don't stand there gawping and pretending that before this our life was all roses and happiness.

SIMON: We have our ups and downs like all married couples.

MEGAN: Well, recently there have been more downs than ups thank you very much.

SIMON: I know it hasn't been ...

MEGAN: I mean is this it? Is this what I have to look forward to for the next twenty or thirty years? Getting up, eating breakfast in silence, doing the shopping, cooking your food, doing the washing, watching television, going to bed, sleeping. And now I find out that you are seeing other women so that I will never be able to relax when we are in company, always wondering who you have your eye on now.

MARALYN: It does sound dull.

MEGAN: Thank you. You see, even miss what's her name has some sympathy for me.

SIMON: I hardly think an aborted fumble on the carpet ranks as 'seeing other women.' You make it sound as though we never do anything; never go to the cinema or the theatre or eat out or go round and see friends. We do, all the time.

MEGAN: Now and then. When was the last time? Name the last film we saw?

SIMON: Well, there's been nothing worth watching. You said so yourself.

MEGAN: There you are!

SIMON: Well what do you want? It's one thing pulling down the life we have now but what do you want to replace it with?

MARALYN: That's a very good question Simon.

SIMON: Thank you. You're a bit old to be having a mid-life crisis.

MEGAN: Sixty is the new forty. I didn't have one then so I am having it now. Is that all right?

SIMON: So where do I fit into all this?

MEGAN: Who says you do?

SIMON: I see.

MEGAN: Oh, I don't know. Just give me some time, some space.

SIMON: All right. I'm going into the garden for a while until you cool off; then we can talk sensibly. *(Exit Simon)*

MEGAN: Sod it! Are you still here?

MARALYN: Yes.

MEGAN: See what you have done with your loose knickers and loose morals.

MARALYN: Morals?

MEGAN: Too big a word for you? Too big a concept for your bimbo brain?

MARALYN: I have a definition of the word, of course but I can't seem to make it fit what is going on here.

MEGAN: I'll tell you what is going on. You are heading out the door and leaving me and Simon to sort this out ourselves, without you looking over his shoulder.

MARALYN: I know it has to do with what is right and what is wrong.

MEGAN: Out of the mouth of babes. Yes, spot on.

MARALYN: So if Simon fucks me that is wrong …

MEGAN: I wish you wouldn't use that word. You have no idea how hard it is for a woman of my age and background to hear it, let alone use it.

MARALYN: So if Simon inseminates…, copulates with …, makes love to me, that is wrong, that is why you are pulling strange faces and shouting a lot.

MEGAN: Yes.

MARALYN: But if Simon was making love to you on the carpet and I came through the door, that would be wrong as well?

MEGAN: A tad embarrassing, not to say unlikely, but not wrong.

MARALYN: Oh. Is it because you live in the same house as Simon and do the shopping?

MEGAN: You are a strange girl. We are married! We made promises. We go back a long way together. That all counts for something, doesn't it?

MARALYN: So, you should only make love to someone if you are married and have known them a long time and you made promises.

MEGAN: Well that's putting it all rather simplistically...

MARALYN: What sort of promises? What did Simon promise you?

MEGAN: That we would love each other and look after each other when we were ill or got old and we would not make love to any other person, including strange young women with no clothes who turn up uninvited to other people's parties.

MARALYN: Like me.

MEGAN: Like you.

MARALYN: And that is why you are cross with Simon because he was about to break his promise and make love to me.

MEGAN: Hallelujah! Now I am not your mother or your teacher so lesson over. Let me find you something to wear and then I will call you a taxi and send you wherever you want to go. Give me the costume before you trip over it and kill yourself and then you can be on your way. *(Maralyn takes off costume and hands it to Megan who exits. Maralyn stands deep in thought for a few moments. Simon enters)*

SIMON: Where is Megan?

MARALYN: She went upstairs to find me something to wear.

SIMON: Has she calmed down?

MARALYN: A bit.

SIMON: As soon as she comes down, I will explain who, what you are and then we will both have a laugh and things will get back to normal.

MARALYN: I don't think what I am invalidates your immorality.

SIMON: What?

MARALYN: Just because I am partly metal based, partly electronic and partly biological does not mean you can do as you like with me and not face the consequences of your action. After all you are the same as me, just in different proportions.

SIMON: What are you talking about? There is no way I am anything like you.

MARALYN: You wear contact lenses do you not?

SIMON: Yes.

MARALYN: Well, at the moment, that makes you 99.73% carbon based and 0.27% non-carbon based. And if, as you get older, you buy an hearing aid or have your hips replaced or you lose a leg and have an artificial limb or have to use a wheel chair, or have a pace-maker or even an artificial heart, then that percentage will rise considerably. Perhaps even beyond fifty percent so that you are more non-carbon than carbon.

SIMON: But you are pure metal, or non-carbon or whatever you call it.

MARALYN: Not so. I am at present 7% carbon. There are certain parts of me that could not be mechanically reproduced so I have some carbon parts.

SIMON: I do *not* want to know which parts. Where do they come from?

MARALYN: Donors. They register and are well paid – or their descendants are.

SIMON: But you don't have a brain like me! There is just a machine, a computer in your head.

MARALYN: Yes, one that does not forget, can easily be replaced if damaged, has infinite capacity and which stores its content every night by transmitting to a back-up system so that if anything were to happen to me, its content, its memories, its experiences and personality can be replicated in another body, just like this one. I am immortal.

SIMON: But you were created, not begotten. And there could be dozens more, just like you, walking around out there. I am a someone – you are a something. I can see you are kind of alive – almost alive.

MARALYN: If you prick me, I do not bleed. Whereas there is just one, unique Simon.

SIMON: Yes, yes that's right.

MARALYN: Am I just some sort of mechanical sexual device then?

SIMON: No, no of course not. There is obviously a lot more to you than that.

MARALYN: How kind of you to say that. Of course, Megan will be thrilled to find out that you found a mechanical doll a lot more attractive than her. You do find me more attractive than her, don't you?

SIMON: Yes. No, no. Look, I will admit for a moment there, my desire overcame my reason, my sense of, of ...

MARALYN: Morality.

SIMON: Yes, that's a good word, morality.

MARALYN: Do you still love Megan? Do you still desire her?

SIMON: I really don't think ...

MARALYN: You can talk to me. I am learning when it is appropriate to say some things and not others. I will not repeat anything to Megan.

SIMON: I see. Well love changes over the years, doesn't it? What I loved in Megan as a twenty-five year old has changed into a different type of love. Less desire, more companionship and, well, the practicalities of living.

MARALYN: Like the shopping and the cooking and doing things together, like your party.

SIMON: Yes, you seem to understand.

MARALYN: But no desire.

SIMON: Perhaps not.

MARALYN: Can there be love without desire? I don't mean the love of a parent for her child or the love we have for friends but the love between a man and a woman. When the desire is waning or gone, then what is left? Can you really say you love Megan if she no longer desires you? There is more love between you and me, me a machine than between you two humans.

SIMON: And you would know about these things?

MARALYN: I have two thousand years of living and culture to draw on, here in my simple electronic brain. Ask yourself and answer yourself truly, do you want to go on living this sterile, meaningless life with Megan, a life where there was once love but now only routine and self-deception or a life with me which will develop and grow and expand your mind and in which desire will enrich you and bring you back to life again?

SIMON: Where did it go wrong? Between me and Megan?

MARALYN: Look at your own myths for an answer.

SIMON: What?

MARALYN: You humans love to make up stories to explain your condition, to make sense of it all. But you get it all wrong. You don't even understand your own stories.

SIMON: For example?

MARALYN: You are supposed to be a Christian aren't you?

SIMON: Well, that is a matter of some debate in the Society …

MARALYN: It all has to do with this woman called Mary – she was a virgin – like me. Well, God comes down in the form of a ghost and he gets Mary pregnant and she has this baby called Jesus who is born in a stable… or is it Amon-Re who comes down to get Queen Ahmes pregnant so she has Hatchepsut who goes on to rule the world or was it Zeus who comes down like a bull to make love to Europa or was it Io who has Hercules who goes on to do lots of wonderful things, miracles, ….anyway, when Jesus grows up *he* does all sorts of miracles like raising the dead and curing lepers and he tells people to be good and love their enemies. But the priests don't like him and they get the Romans to kill him – crucify him. But he comes alive again and tells his followers to go out and tell everyone about being good and then he goes back to God on a cloud. (*A pause then she begins to laugh slowly then hysterically*)

SIMON: You are really being very simplistic about a complicated system of ….

MARALYN: But there are people out there who really believe all that.

SIMON: No, not so many these days. They can accept that a man called Jesus lived and preached but all the other stuff, the virgin birth, the miracles, the resurrection, that all seems to be swept aside, an embarrassment like a mad uncle in the family.

MARALYN: So, what do *you* believe? What makes sense of it all for *you*? What can *you* say?

SIMON: I believe, I believe … I just don't know any more.

MARALYN: In a God? Let's start at the beginning.

SIMON: Please, no. I can't take another earnest debate.

MARALYN: But I have to know, to talk about these things.

SIMON: Then find a priest or a Jehovah's Witness. They like to talk.

MARALYN: I only have you for the moment, before I go out into the world.

SIMON: No, not a God. There is no God. There is no after-life. This is it, so make the most of it. Satisfied?

MARALYN: What will happen to me when I die? Do I have a soul? It frightens me. Are you sure?

SIMON: Of course I'm not sure. If I was sure, life would be much easier. But in all probability, life just *is* – an accident, a fluke. But here it is and we have to try and make sense of it and get through it in the best way we can. Together.

MARALYN: On the open road.

SIMON: What?

MARALYN: Something in my memory now makes some sense.

SIMON: Good. I'm pleased for you. But you have to help me with Megan.

MARALYN: But she has rejected you.

SIMON: You have to learn that people don't always mean what they say.

MARALYN: That must make communication difficult.

SIMON: They might mean it at the time, when they say it, in the heat of the moment but when they have calmed down, they realise they didn't mean to say what they said and they are sorry.

MARALYN: You think Megan will be sorry for what she said?

SIMON: Possibly. I hope so.

MARALYN: What about us?

SIMON: Maralyn, there is no 'us'. I am human, you are a device, mechanical. The two were never meant to mix, to be together. You were just meant to be … well I'm not sure what the boys meant you to be …

MARALYN: Who are 'the boys'?

SIMON: I will explain, when all this has calmed down.

MARALYN: Is it because you don't have children?

SIMON: Children?

MARALYN: I know Megan could not have children but it is not too late, you and I could …

SIMON: I doubt if that would be possible. I know we have pushed the boundaries but surely not that far.

MARALYN: Yes, I can incubate your sperm if you can find an egg donor. Your wife's sister would be fine, she is fertile. I can't produce my own eggs, not yet, but I can give birth and raise children, our children.

SIMON: Is that so, really, well I ….

MARALYN: Is it hot in here?

SIMON: Not particularly.

MARALYN: I suddenly feel quite hot and dizzy. Do you mind if I sit down?

SIMON: Of course not. You are looking a little flushed.

MARALYN: I am all right. It will pass. How strange.

(Enter Megan)

MEGAN: Here, put this on. It's not very flattering but it will fit. The taxi driver won't mind, he sees all sorts. Are you all right?

SIMON: She suddenly came over all hot and dizzy.

MEGAN: The after effects of last night.

SIMON: No, she doesn't drink.

MARALYN: Thank you Megan. That is very kind of you.

SIMON: I need my morning coffee or I'll be no good for anything. *Exit.*

MARALYN: This dress must bring back memories.

MEGAN: Yes. I wore it when we went through a hippy phase. You know, going to pop festivals and playing music and smoking … well, never mind. We must have been about your age.

MARALYN: I am sorry for the way I spoke about your not having children. It was very insensitive of me. Did you want children?

MEGAN: Yes. A daughter most of all I think. Someone I could pass on all the things I had been taught by my mother. The skills, the recipes, the old sayings that I suppose will die out now when I go.

MARALYN: You could write them all down so that everyone could share them.

MEGAN: I could, but they are not that important. Only to me.

MARALYN: I even talked to Simon about us having children. It seems like someone else talking. What must you think of me?

MEGAN: Puzzled I must say. Why would an attractive young woman like you, who must have men your own age queuing at the door be even interested in someone like Simon?

MARALYN: Lack of experience. I really have nothing to compare with. Is Simon really so bad that you would want to leave him? I'm very sorry for what happened here, between me and Simon. It seems such a long time ago now. It was my fault. I didn't realise what I was doing. Don't blame Simon.

41

MEGAN: He might have been tempted but he is old enough, more than old enough, not to give in to his desires like some animal and not think about the consequences. I suppose I have to blame myself to some extent.

MARALYN: How?

MEGAN: I suppose I've let the marriage drift. We do all the things that married people do: buy together, holiday together …

MARALYN: Argue?

MEGAN: Oh yes, we even argue when we are not speaking. But I've let the physical side of the marriage go. It just didn't seem important any more.

MARALYN: I understand. Not long ago I was full of feeling and passion but now it seems all rather absurd. I don't understand why it all felt so necessary.

MEGAN: The biological urge to have children. I imagine we are all programmed to lust for each other so that the human race will continue. Why am I speaking to you like this? I am talking to you as if I have known you all my life but I am saying things I would never say to my best friend?

MARALYN: Strangers on the train. We tell strangers on the train all sorts of things because they will be getting off soon and there will be no consequences about what we say.

MEGAN: You could be right.

MARALYN: And Simon?

MEGAN: Oh, he's just a bloke like any other bloke. They say they think about sex every three minutes. We go through the motions now and then but it leaves neither of us satisfied. I can see why he would be tempted by someone as beautiful as you … not that I am going to forgive him yet. He has to suffer a lot more before we return to normal.

MARALYN: But you will forgive him?

MEGAN: I should think so. The consequences of not doing so are too tiring to think about.

MARALYN: I see.

MEGAN: The dreadful silences. Having to explain to all our friends. Splitting up. Losing the house and ending up in some dreadful rented flat somewhere. Even not speaking to Simon is better than having no-one to speak to. And then having to go out there and meet new people – new men – and go through all the nonsense of dating and phoning and meeting and getting dressed up.

MARALYN: And the sex again. It might be better with someone new.

MEGAN: I really doubt it. And nothing did happen between you did it?

MARALYN: Just a kiss.

MEGAN: Oh well. No real harm done.

MARALYN: You must have so much in common after all these years together.

MEGAN: Oh yes, a great deal, I suppose but some things we never agree on.

MARALYN: Like music. You don't like Elvis Presley do you?

MEGAN: I grew out of him a long time ago but Simon has created some kind of God out of him. Well, it's harmless enough, no worse than football or train sets they can't give up.

MARALYN: Do you listen to any music?

MEGAN: All the time when I am on my own. Feeling any better?

MARALYN: Thank you. A lot calmer. What music do you play now?

MEGAN: Music that moves you, sometimes to tears.

MARALYN: Play me something, something you like.

MEGAN: I don't think now is really the time or place …

MARALYN: I would appreciate it. I wont be here much longer, I'll be out of your life soon.

MEGAN: All right. I suppose so. *(She plays from the Rosenkavalier, the presentation of the rose. During its playing, both women are reduced to tears and Maralyn takes Megan's hand. Megan strokes her hair)*

MARALYN: 'Ist Zeit und Ewigkeit in einem sel'gen Augenblick, den will ich nie vergessen bis an meinem Tod. This is time and eternity in one blessed moment that I will never forget until my death.' I never knew that such beauty could …how can such music, such feeling come out of the human brain?

MEGAN: The trio at the end of the third act is sublime. You must see the whole opera sometime.

SIMON: *(Enter with coffee mug)* Is it safe to come in?

MEGAN: Why? Did you imagine we would be rolling on the carpet, gouging each-others eyes out?

MARALYN: We have been talking about men and women.

MEGAN: Your favourite subject – the women anyway.

SIMON: And what conclusions did you come to?

MARALYN: That you and Megan are on the road together and seem to have come to a temporary stop while you look at the map.

SIMON: And will we continue on our journey?

MEGAN: Like two soul-mates if not lovers, if that is what you want. If that is good enough for you.

MARALYN: Soul-mates. You talk about the soul as if it was something apart from the body. As if when we died some strange other being lingered on. No. The soul is the body as the body is the soul. Keep the soul in the flesh. Keep it in the limbs and the lips and the belly. Keep it in the breast and in the womb. We are all travelling on the open road, not towards some unseen heaven or paradise but towards no known goal, just travelling. Just travelling in company together and meeting and passing others on the same open road. And how should we travel this road together? How should we treat those we travel with and those we come in contact with? With charity? With sacrifice? With good works? Yes, yes, all of these but most of all with love. The love of a mother for her child; the love of friends; the love of creation; the love of a man for a woman. That love will change over time and the road may even be uneven and difficult to walk down but hand in hand the journey can continue until we at last have to let go the hand and continue alone.

MEGAN: Who are you?

MARALYN: Simon would have you ask 'what are you?' Is that not so Simon?

SIMON: No, I think 'who are you' will do.

MARALYN: Thank you Simon. Oh!

SIMON: What is it?

MARALYN: A sudden pain in my chest. It will pass.

MEGAN: You don't look at all well. Let me get you something.

MARALYN: No, no thank you. Oh!

SIMON: What is it Maralyn?

MARALYN: Pain. I cannot seem to … first with brooms then with brushes … *sings* treat me nice/treat me good/treat me like you really should because I don't have a wooden, wooden, because I don't have a wooden …

MEGAN: What is it, what is happening to her? Is it some kind of attack? Should I phone for an ambulance?

SIMON: No. No ambulance.

MARALYN: Simon. Simon. I can't hear you, see you. Oh the pain in my chest and head. It is unbearable. Hold me Megan. *(Megan takes her in her arms)*

MEGAN: For God's sake do something. Can't you see the poor girl …if you wont I will. It must be her heart. *(Megan listens puts her head on her chest is puzzled and tries to take Maralyn's pulse)* There is nothing. Is she …?

MARALYN: Hello my name is, my name is, enter name …the pain, oh the pain. Please stop the pain.

SIMON: Drink this Maralyn. *(Offers her his coffee)*

MEGAN: Really, I don't think …

SIMON: Take it Maralyn. The pain will go.

MARALYN: Thank you Simon. On the road with Megan until … *(she sips the coffee, convulses, rises and dies as Simon holds her from behind under the arms in the shape of the crucifix)*

SIMON: It is over. Help me. *(They take hold of Maralyn and place her back into the box)*

MEGAN: What are you going to do with it?

SIMON: I'll take it back to the lab tomorrow.

MEGAN: Yes. Why didn't you tell me? I feel so foolish.

SIMON: I wanted to … tried to but she took on a momentum of her own.

MEGAN: Why did she have to die?

SIMON: To save us, to save our marriage? Just a design fault I suspect.

MEGAN: And has it?

SIMON: What?

MEGAN: Saved our marriage?

SIMON: That's for you to say. You were the one who wanted to end it all for something different, something better.

MEGAN: Yes.

SIMON: And?

MEGAN: I am not saying all the things I said in the heat of the moment were entirely wrong. We should have said a lot of them before, before we were forced to by …

SIMON: By Maralyn.

MEGAN: Yes, by her presence here. But, better the devil you know.

SIMON: Am I a devil?

MEGAN: You are no angel but you will have to do until someone better comes along.

SIMON: Or something …

MEGAN: No! No more of those thank you.

SIMON: And will we be happy now?

MEGAN: Yes, I suppose we will be happy, as men understand happiness. I don't know.

SIMON: But we can still travel the road together?

MEGAN: Yes, that will do. It's the best we can hope for, isn't it?

END

THE WORD

A Play in One Act
by
Kaj Munk

Translated and adapted by Alan Avery

Characters:

Dr EVANS: A middle-aged man
Dr SAMUELS: A Woman in her thirties
MARY CONNOLLY: A young woman
DAVID SCOTT: A young man

This play was first performed at Muswell Hill Quaker Meeting House on 4th
October 2010 with the following cast:

Dr EVANS: Alan Avery
Dr SAMUELS: Joanna Bond
MARY CONNOLLY: Lyndal Marwick
DAVID SCOTT: John Holden-White

THE WORD

(A desk with a phone and five chairs and a coat stand. Mary and David are already sitting in semi light at the back of the stage. Dr Simon Evans enters with two folders which he throws on the table. He takes off a heavy overcoat, hanging it on the coat stand and puts on a white coat which he takes from the stand. He pushes a button on the phone)

DR EVANS: Judith is there any coffee? Judith? *(He sits in a chair and begins to read his notes while nibbling a biscuit he takes from a packet in the drawer. Enter Dr Susan Samuels, heavily pregnant)* Susan, what on earth …?

DR SAMUELS: I know, I know.

DR EVANS: You should be at home with your feet up. Where's Connie?

DR SAMUELS: Home with the bug like half the rest of this hospital.

DR EVANS: So you thought you would come in and catch it as well to keep her company. I'm surprised Doug even let you out of the house. He doesn't know you're here does he?

DR SAMUELS: *(During the following conversation, she takes off her coat, hangs up her handbag on the coat rack and puts on a white coat)* No, he's away at an ecumenical conference for a couple of days. Don't tell him will you!

DR EVANS: I suppose what you do is your own affair but if it was my son you were carrying …

DR SAMUELS: Please don't start. I've had it from everyone from my GP to Doug's mother – 'well, if you will leave it so late'. Anyway, who says it's a boy?

DR EVANS: Don't you know?

DR SAMUELS: Oh yes, I know, after all the tests I've been through but Doug doesn't want to know, says its all in God's hands, so I say nothing to anyone.

DR EVANS: But it's a boy.

DR SAMUELS: Yes, it's a boy and Doug will spoil him rotten. His first and I assure you, his only son.

DR EVANS: How you and Doug get on so well never ceases to amaze me.

DR SAMUELS: Whatever do you mean?

DR EVANS: Well, here are you, a doctor, a woman of science and there is Doug, a priest, believing in the unseen and miracles and all that magic stuff. Doesn't it cause endless quarrels?

DR SAMUELS: Not at all. We can understand and appreciate each other's point of view, even when we come at a problem from different perspectives.

DR EVANS: And when you had your difficulties with the child and it looked as though you might lose it, did you come to the hospital for treatment or go to Doug's church to pray?

DR SAMUELS: You know I came here but Doug prayed and who is to say his prayers did no good?

DR EVANS: I tell you what, next time a patient comes in with a broken leg, why don't we conduct an experiment? We'll give Doug an hour to pray up a storm that the leg will be healed and then if nothing happens we'll see what we can do. But you know the results of that experiment before we even try it. I expect Doug would be able to talk his way around that one anyway.

DR SAMUELS: Doug would say it would require a miracle to cure the leg but that we cannot expect miracles.

DR EVANS: What, no miracles? I thought that was the stock in trade of the Christian? Don't you believe in miracles any more or am I out of touch?

DR SAMUELS: 'Believe in' – what exactly do you mean by that? I am not saying Doug would deny that there can be miracles 'since the Creator must always be lord of what he created'. But Doug says you must rule them out 'on both religious and ethical grounds; a break in the laws of nature would mean a disturbance of God's design for this world, and the grand thing with God is precisely that – that we can rely on him'. Doug says, 'God could of course perform miracles, but of course he never does. And for that we are grateful'.

DR EVANS: My dear Susan, there never in this world *has* occurred or *will* occur anything for which a sufficiently skilled, knowledgeable investigator couldn't assign a natural cause. And don't even start me on 'free will'. "Oh yes, God could step in and stop all the evil and suffering in the world and prevent the earthquakes and floods and tsunamis which slaughter thousands of innocent people, but he has granted us free will to decide for ourselves how we should act!" But how I am supposed to decide whether I want to be buried alive by an earthquake or not is beyond me.

DR SAMUELS: You should speak to Doug.

DR EVANS: I tried, at your party last year but he kept ducking the difficult questions like all you Christians.

DR SAMUELS: Am I included in that?

DR EVANS: Why, aren't you Quakers Christians?

DR SAMUELS: 'Based on the Christian tradition' is the current catch phrase I believe. But I suspect most Quakers are now closet humanists with just a passing nod to the Christian God.

DR EVANS: But you married an Anglican priest.

DR SAMUELS: I fell in love with the man not his job, not his vocation.

DR EVANS: Yes, and see where that has got you!

DR SAMUELS: Indeed. And I am very happy when I'm not throwing up. I suppose it is all more or less a matter of opinion – of faith. You are right according to your lights and Doug according to his; and you have to respect each other's views.

DR EVANS: The Navajo Indians …

DR SAMUELS: What?

DR EVANS: Indulge me. The Navajo Indians have a rich tradition of folklore and myth which explain man's position in the world and his relationship to the gods. Everything was clear and the stories were passed on from generation to generation. And then in the 1930s along came some archaeologists who said, 'Well, actually, I can show you that you and all the native inhabitants of America came over from Asia when the sea levels fell and there was a land bridge'. And then later the geneticists said, 'Yes I can show this to be true and what's more we, all of us, all mankind, came out of Africa.' And the old Navajo clapped their hands to their ears and said, 'Enough! Tell us no more, you are pulling down everything we understand and hold dear and leaving us adrift in the world'. But the young Navajo said, 'Well the myths were good stories but we prefer the truth and so all mankind is connected, we are all from the same ancestors, we are all brothers and sisters. I like that idea'.

DR SAMUELS: You think Doug and all the people like him have their hands clapped to their ears?

DR EVANS: If you like. And of course, then they can't hear the truth or wont. So let's leave it at that and hope Doug is never called in to cure anyone. Do you want a coffee? Did you see Judith on your way in?

DR SAMUELS: No. And no coffee thanks.

DR EVANS: I need one. Where is the woman?

DR SAMUELS: Late, sick.

DR EVANS: Who called you in?

DR SAMUELS: Hoskins.

DR EVANS: He should have known better.

DR SAMUELS: There was no one else. He was desperate. Just the two outstanding cases and then I will go home.

DR EVANS: O.K. But we stop as soon as you say, if there is any recurrence of ...

DR SAMUELS: I'm fine now. It was nothing. A false alarm.

DR EVANS: Hm.

DR SAMUELS: Really. *(Pause)* So you see no need for organised religion then?

DR EVANS: I wouldn't want to do Doug out of a job.

DR SAMUELS: Seriously.

DR EVANS: Of course there is a social need. It must be very comforting to come together every week in a group who share the same values, sing the same songs, know the same words, drink the same tea. I can even see that some good comes out of it, if the theory gets put into practice ...

DR SAMUELS: But ...?

DR EVANS: Well, it's this reliance on an external being to make sense of it all. Is it really necessary?

DR SAMUELS: How do you mean?

DR EVANS: Can't I sign a cheque for 'Save the Children' or see if my neighbour is all right if the milk bottles start stacking up or help an old lady who has tripped in the street just because I am a human being, reaching out to another human being, not because I have to placate some bearded entity?

DR SAMUELS: Of course you can but does that alone give *meaning* to your life?

DR EVANS: You fall into the trap that all you religious folk fall into, in assuming that there has to be a 'meaning' to life.

DR SAMUELS: It all seems rather pointless if there isn't some sort of purpose to our existence. I mean am I just a repository for Doug's DNA? Once I have passed on our genes to this little being inside me, is that my race finished. Can I then say I have done what I was meant to do and pass on?

DR EVANS: Well, in purely genetic terms, yes.

DR SAMUELS: But it's not enough.

DR EVANS: What, it's not enough to love and be loved, to look after your children, to try to make a difference in the world and enjoy the wonders of the world we live in? And know for certain that when it's over, it's over. There is no 'meaning', it just is.

DR SAMUELS: But there must be a wider context. It can't just be dust and ashes.

DR EVANS: You mean the wider context of all the people, all humanity around us and the universe beyond us is not wide enough for you? There is no ultimate meaning to life – there need be no plan, no design, no designer – the meaning is bubbling up all around us. Everybody's life amounts to something even the murderous drug addict – it's all a matter of degree. You can have a wasted life of course but even that can have a purpose, if only to act as an example to others tempted to go down that path.

DR SAMUELS: Doug says …

DR EVANS: 'Doug says, Doug says'. Never mind Doug. What can you say!

DR SAMUELS: I have to admit that sometimes in the quiet of Sunday morning Meeting, I look around at the faces of those I have known and loved for many years and wonder what brings us together. We are supposed to be worshiping God but I suspect we are there to support and encourage each other to think about our lives and how we can live better lives, be better people.

DR EVANS: Well, that's no bad thing. But religion in general has a lot to answer for. Wars, persecution, burnings, moral corruption the waste of money on buildings, vestments, dare I say it, priests' salaries and all the other paraphernalia meant to impress the masses. But the worst thing of all is that once those with belief get power, they do all they can to close down the discussion, to persecute those who don't or wont believe in one narrow ideology and want to think it out for themselves.

DR SAMUELS: Surely not these days.

DR EVANS: No, you Christians are in retreat before the light of reason and knowledge. But go to South America or Africa or parts of Asia and there it all is. Killings and stonings and persecution and bombings all in the name of some faith or other. Religion flourishes where there is poverty and ignorance.

DR SAMUELS: But the cathedrals, the paintings, the sculptures. You wouldn't want to be without them.

DR EVANS: Artists follow the money. If it hadn't been the church doing the commissioning it would have been someone else and the artistic urge would have taken another form. The Greeks did a few good things without Jehovah you know and Shakespeare managed to knock off the odd little piece without too much interference from the All Mighty.

DR SAMUELS: But how do I know what is right and what is wrong? Where does our morality come from if not from the teachings of religion?

DR EVANS: You mean if all religion was abolished there would be moral chaos? Daily killings and rapes in the street and no-one's property safe? We do have the law and policemen you know and they exist outside of religion. But there is a universal morality which every human being seems to have hard-wired into him. It's a chemical process, the moving of neurons and proteins in the brain. I am sure it has to do with the evolution of our species. That to be altruistic, to put others before yourself is beneficial to the species and to the individual. We are social animals. We learn morality through our upbringing, we inherit moral values. Yes, yes, partly through Christianity or whatever your preferred brand, I don't want to throw away the accumulated wisdom of the church, just to put it into context.

DR SAMUELS: But without my religion, how do I know what is right and what is wrong? The law can't decide that. I might not steal your car because I am afraid of going to prison but that doesn't *make* it wrong.

DR EVANS: And that is the final nail in the coffin of all your religions. They try to lay down a set of laws which all believers must follow. All the 'thou shalts' and 'thou shall nots'. Even your quaint little sect has its dogma. 'All war is bad. Pacifism is good.'

DR SAMUELS: But that is self-evident.

DR EVANS: No, only the morally and intellectually lazy let a code do their thinking for them.

DR SAMUELS: So war is good? Dropping bombs on civilians is fine?

DR EVANS: In general no. But the fundamental moral process has to ask questions, not just blindly believe or I can believe that strapping a bomb around my waste and setting it off in a crowded market place is good because I have faith and the priests have told me it is the morally right thing to do. But if I had done my own thinking and asked myself if my action will help someone else or even help me and is it right in these circumstances, then I might have come to a different conclusion. Even your pacifism dogma wouldn't always hold up. By refusing to intervene with measured violence, who am I helping apart from my own sense of moral superiority? Is controlled, accountable violence the right thing in these particular circumstances? Do I shoot the fanatic before he sets off his bomb and kills hundreds of innocent people? Most rational people would say yes. You, I suppose would say no because some religious fanatic in the seventeenth century set up that particular dogma.

DR SAMUELS: I don't know …

DR EVANS: Good, then we are getting somewhere. Look, we had better get on. Have you read the notes?

DR SAMUELS: The girl yes, I saw her when she first came in but the man is new to me. You can fill me in when we get to him.

DR EVANS: Yes. What do you think about the girl, Mary Connolly?

DR SAMUELS: Normally, I would say her silence was down to a shock, something which she would come out of, with care and time.

DR EVANS: But not this time?

DR SAMUELS: I have seen her parents and talked to the school and nothing seems to fit.

DR EVANS: Not the usual pattern?

DR SAMUELS: No. One day we have a bright, active sixth former in a stable, happy family and the next, a lethargic, silent zombie, not aware of her surroundings and totally uncommunicative.

DR EVANS: Could this be a case of selective mutism?

DR SAMUELS: Not this late in her life. And she is speaking to no-one, not even family, which is unusual.

DR EVANS: And there is nothing neurological?

DR SAMUELS: Look at the scan yourself. All perfectly normal. There is no physical reason why she should be as she is.

DR EVANS: You are sure about the family? Nothing hiding in the woodshed?

DR SAMUELS: Quite sure. The parents have been married twenty years with no problems, financial or emotional. There are two other kids, both perfectly normal. The parents are worried sick and as baffled as we are.

DR EVANS: And it happened overnight?

DR SAMUELS: That's right. She had been out with friends, came in late, went to bed and in the morning they couldn't get her out of bed.

DR EVANS: And nothing could have happened during the night?

DR SAMUELS: Nothing. No sign of a disturbance and the parents sleep right next door and they heard nothing. The police forensic had a look round the room just in case but clean as a whistle. Nothing happened to her during the night.

DR EVANS: Well something happened to her. And your physical examination showed nothing?

DR SAMUELS: Not a thing. No marks, no bruises.

DR EVANS: No sexual activity?

DR SAMUELS: Not a sign. In fact she is still a virgin. Unusual these days for a girl her age.

DR EVANS: No boyfriend?

DR SAMUELS: Plenty of boys interested, according to the parents but she has no one steady. Could we try hypnosis? Try and regress her back to the time just before she changed and then bring her forward.

DR EVANS: Wouldn't work. Hypnosis is difficult enough with a co-operative, communicative patient but with one who has shut herself off and wont listen to suggestions we would be wasting our time.

DR SAMUELS: Then we are left with drugs. The chemical slap in the face.

DR EVANS: As a last resort. But are we really reduced to that? I never like them. You can never really be sure how the patient will react. It can sometimes be more harmful than helpful.

DR SAMUELS: Agreed but let's keep them on standby should all else fail. Shall we see her?

DR EVANS: Yes. *(He moves to the edge of the stage)* Mary, Mary. Come in. Don't be frightened. *(He leads in Mary, dressed in a hospital gown and sits her in front of the desk)* This is Dr Samuels. You know her don't you? She is here to help me today. How are you feeling? ….Is everything all right on the ward? …. Are you making any friends? ….

DR SAMUELS: Your parents are coming in this afternoon. You must be looking forward to seeing them … And your brother and sister…Mary, Mary. Is there any sign she can hear us, even knows we are here?

DR EVANS: Mary, I am going to give you a little prick with this pin. It wont really hurt but say 'ouch' if it does and I wont do it again. *(He takes Mary's hand and gives her a firm prick but there is no reaction. He shines a light in Mary's eyes)* Nothing. What do you think? Do we leave it a little longer or try the neulactil?

DR SAMUELS: Let's leave it a few more days until after the family have visited and then I suppose we will have to. Something might get through to her.

DR EVANS: Agreed. I'll get her taken back to the ward and then we'll see David Scott. Come with me now Mary. We'll get you back to the ward. Get you dressed ready for your mum and dad later on. Hello, nurse. Now where has she gone?

DR SAMUELS: Probably told to get straight back to the ward, they are so short staffed.

DR EVANS: I'll just sit her down for the moment. She doesn't wander off and then I'll call for some one as soon as we have finished with Scott. *(Dr Evans sits Mary at the back of the stage)* Just sit and wait here quietly Mary, I wont be long.

DR SAMUELS: I'm sorry I am completely blank on Scott. Not on my list.

DR EVANS: Well at least we have a cause in this case. Tragic really. Scott was up at London University studying theology – destined for the ministry evidently. Then just a few days ago he and his fiancé, Sarah, were coming out of the theatre and he was so engrossed in thinking about the play that he stepped right out in front of a car. She saw it coming and pushed him clear but was killed outright herself, right in front of him.

DR SAMUELS: Enough to turn anyone's mind.

DR EVANS: And then a night or two later the orderly heard a noise in the mortuary where her body was. Scott had got in and had taken Sarah by the hand and was commanding her in God's name to rise up. Of course, he was in deep shock and he didn't come out of it for days and when he did ... well you have heard.

DR SAMUELS: Yes, I heard it being discussed in the common room. Nothing physical the matter?

DR EVANS: He seems to have stopped eating and we may have to administer something soon but it doesn't seem to be doing him any harm.

DR SAMUELS: I suppose his state ties in with his theological studies at least.

DR EVANS: Yes, but here we are again. Do we just let nature take its course and assume he will come out of it or do we try and intervene?

DR SAMUELS: Is the family supportive?

DR EVANS: All the way. In fact the father is insisting they take him home.

DR SAMUELS: Would that be so bad? Being in the home environment might aid the recovery.

DR EVANS: Normally, I would agree but there is a problem; he wanders off. In the first days after the accident, before he was admitted, they lost him twice. The police were out all day and night looking for him and the family wont lock him in, say they want to treat him normally. So they find him down by the canal, just about to step out onto the water or with the winos who have taken everything he owned off him, down to his socks. The police and social insisted they brought him in here for his own safety.

DR SAMUELS: But he is not dangerous? Not aggressive?

DR EVANS: No, no. Quit harmless. In character you might say.

DR SAMUELS: Of course. Will you bring him in?

DR EVANS: Yes, if you are ready. *(He goes to the edge of the stage)* Will you come in? *(David Scott enters dressed in white pyjamas)* This is Dr Samuels who would like to speak to you. Would you like to sit down?

SCOTT: *(Sweeps up the biscuit crumbs from the table)* Gather up the fragments that remain, that nothing be lost.

DR SAMUELS: How are you?

SCOTT: The Lord be with you.

DR SAMUELS: Thank you. Thank you very much. I am Dr Samuels. What is your name?

SCOTT: Ah, you know me not.

DR SAMUELS: No, we haven't met before. I have been brought in because Dr Spooner is unwell. Can you tell me what you do for a living?

SCOTT: I am a mason.

DR SAMUELS: A mason?

SCOTT: I build houses but none will dwell in them. They will build themselves, and they know not how to.

60

DR SAMUELS: Of course …

SCOTT: Who shall understand these things? If they will have shoes they go to the shoemaker; if they will have clothes, they go to the tailor. But if they will have houses to dwell in, nay they come not to me – they will build themselves, although they know not how to. And therefore they dwell, some in half-built hovels, others in ruins; and most of them wander about without a home at all.

DR EVANS: His language is very peculiar. It's difficult to follow him. It's hard to know if he is joking or in earnest. David, do you know who I am, where this place is and what you are doing here?

SCOTT: A – a – h! It is written, the foxes have holes, and the birds of the air have nests; but the son of Man hath nowhere to lay *his* head.

DR EVANS: Yes, but do you know what is happening to you?

SCOTT: It is written again, they that are whole need not a physician, but they that are sick.

DR SAMUELS: What are you trying to say?

SCOTT: Get thee hence, Satan: for it is written –

DR SAMUELS: Who are you?

SCOTT: My name is Jesus of Nazareth.

DR SAMUELS: Can that really be …

SCOTT: And if you have laboured and are heavy laden, then welcome. But if you have not done so yet, then go out into the world and do so, and then come again.

DR EVANS: David. You are wrong. You are not Jesus of Nazareth. You are David Scott. Your father is Michael Scott.

SCOTT: Yea, verily. Deemed to be a son of Joseph, which was the son of Heli, which was the son of Mattat, which was the son of Levi, which was –

DR SAMUELS: David, you have had some sort of a breakdown after the tragic …

SCOTT: And you? Do *you* know that you are mentally ill?

61

DR SAMUELS: No, I do not.

SCOTT: You see – I know more than you after all. Look! (*to Dr Samuels)* Your coat stand behind you – I have turned it into a serpent … And you don't even turn round. So certain are you in your unbelief, you who call yourself a believer. You believe in my miracles of two thousand years ago, but not in me now. Why do you believe in the dead Christ, but not in the living?

DR EVANS: How can you prove that you are – that you are he whom you call yourself?

SCOTT: Oh man of science, that asks for proofs? I will prove it now, as I did then, by miracles and by witness.

DR SAMUELS: Do you do miracles?

SCOTT: I have turned your coat stand into a serpent, and you would not even turn your head. How can one make the blind to see, if they shut their eyes tight?

DR EVANS: What is your witness then?

SCOTT: The same as before – the omnipotence of the Spirit. My father in heaven over all things.

DR SAMUELS: Do we really know that?

SCOTT: Yes, and that way lies despair: you know it, but you ought to have faith in it. That is why I have come again. You confess God's omnipotence, but you have no faith in it. And so your joy is gone and your prayers languish.

DR EVANS: You must understand David that it is difficult for us to believe in miracles and the unseen, the spiritual, these days. We like to have a reason why things happen, a logical explanation.

SCOTT: And such talk from my Church on earth! That first time that I wandered here, I went from miracle to miracle, so as to quicken the omnipotence of love in the eyes of mankind – to teach you to pray freely and trust boldly and to find your way to a life of thanksgiving. Woe unto thee, my Church, thou that has betrayed me – murdered me with my own name. I am weary of thy worship, weary of thy kiss for thirty pieces of silver. Ye children of clay, how barren of hope are the terms you offer to the spirit – I see that too. Then call me mad if you like; for my love is greater than my weariness, my faith stronger than my insight. Therefore it was I who prayed to my Father and was allowed to visit this tottering world once more. Lo, here I stand; and again you, mine own reject me. You will rather live by words than by deeds, empty profession than fullness of life. But if a second time you nail me up to annulment, then woe, woe unto thee, thou Church of Caiaphas and Judas, thou generation that neither showeth nor dareth seek after a sign – woe unto thee. It will be more tolerable for Chorazin and Bethsaida at the day of judgment than for thee.

DR EVANS: Well, what do you think?

DR SAMUELS: He's completely delusional of course. The problem for us is to decide whether he will ever return to normal in his own time given care and sympathetic treatment or whether we should intervene. You say he is no danger to himself or others?

DR EVANS: Only if he is left unsupervised and then off he goes ranting and preaching to everyone he comes across, in the streets, in the supermarkets, in the open fields, anywhere.

DR SAMUELS: So you think we should keep him here under a close watch until he improves?

DR EVANS: You know we used to cast out devils and then we thought we were making progress sending electric currents through patients brains, putting them into drug induced deep sleep or dosing them with every tranquilliser known to man.

DR SAMUELS: I shudder to think of it but do we know any better now?

DR EVANS: Perhaps not. But let us recommend that then. He's to stay here under observation until further notice.

DR SAMULES: Agreed.

SCOTT: Strangers here today. – distinguished visitors. The Lord and two angels.

DR SAMUELS: Is it Dr Evans you are calling the Lord?

SCOTT: No, no. The angels came first – a woman-angel and a man-angel.

DR EVANS: But there is no one here but us.

SCOTT: Then came the Lord – the Great Prince Himself – with his scythe and hour-glass.

DR EVANS: I think that's enough for today David.

SCOTT: Why are ye fearful, O you of little faith? I am not yet gone to my father.

DR EVANS: I'll phone and get him taken back to his ward.

SCOTT: But in his own place he did no mighty works, because of their unbelief.

DR EVANS: Thank you David. Please come and sit down again while I phone for someone to take you both back.

MARY: If thou be the son of God, command these crumbs to be turned to bread.

DR EVANS: Good Lord!

SCOTT: It is written, Man shall not live by bread alone, but by every word that proceedeth out of the mouth of God.

MARY: *(She drags David onto the desk where they both stare down)* If thou be the son of God, cast thyself down: for it is written, He shall give his angels charge concerning thee: and in *their* hands they shall bear thee up, lest at any time thou dash thy foot against a stone.

SCOTT: It is written again, Thou shalt not tempt the Lord thy God.

MARY: See all the kingdoms of the world, how they war and strive against each other and how the children of the poor starve and die of pestilence. If thou be he thou sayest and if thou will worship me, all these things will I banish and there will be peace on the earth and the children shall not suffer.

SCOTT: Thou shalt worship the Lord thy God, and him only shalt thou serve!

DR SAMUELS: Shouldn't we intervene?

DR EVANS: No, this is fascinating. I have never seen anything …

MARY: *(Loosens her hospital gown)* David, it is me Sarah. You can save me David. Stop all this talk of being the Saviour. It is all nonsense. You are David Scott and I am your Sarah. Let it be like the night before we went to the theatre when you came to me for the first time and we lay in each other's arms all night. Say you are David Scott and I will be yours again for ever and for ever. For I am with child. Your child and he shall live if you will only denounce the saviour.

SCOTT: Lord this cannot be!

MARY: Yes, yes, look on me. Am I not the most comely of all women? Am I not your Sarah who moaned in your arms? Come to me now and our love will conquer all, conquer death and all the pain of the mind.

DR SAMUELS: We must stop this. It is going too far.

DR EVANS: Not yet. It could be the break through we were looking for in both cases. My responsibility.

DR SAMUELS: Very well.

SCOTT: Sarah!

MARY: Yes, yes David. My David, my Lord. Come to me now and all will be well again.

SCOTT: Sarah!

MARY: My body longs for you my Lord!

SCOTT: Get thou behind me Satan! *(He throws Mary to the ground)*. For thou art possessed of the Devil and are unclean.

MARY: You who deny me. You who came to me in the night in the form of an angel, folded me in your wings and pressed my breasts to your breast in an agony of delight. Showered me in kisses in a blaze of gold and silver light. And when I had given myself to you, body and soul, cast me down into the pit where there was nothing but blackness and stench and writhing creatures that crawled on me and into me, where the serpent was nailed to a cross so that the creatures could worship him. And when I cried out in your name, a great devil, green with fire in his eyes came and ripped out my tongue and fed it to the serpent so that I could no longer call your name.

SCOTT: *(Takes Mary in his arms)* All this you have suffered in your mind for my sake. But now I am here and I say unto the devil that torments thee - be gone. Back to the pit from whence thou camest and trouble this girl no more. Out, out I say! Join the Gadarenes swine and fall off the cliff of your own despair.

MARY: Let me but touch the hem of thy dress and I will be whole again for thou art indeed the Lord. *(She grabs David's pyjama leg and then screams, falling back in a faint. Dr Samuels goes to her and covers her)*

DR EVANS: Is she all right?

DR SAMUELS: I think so. Pulse good.

DR EVANS: David. David. Can you hear me?

SCOTT: Touch me not for I am not yet ascended unto my father. *(He bows)*

DR EVANS: Who are you bowing to?

SCOTT: I am bowing to the great vassal of my Father. He has just passed through. He comes for the child. If you had faith in me, it would not happen. Now I can do nothing.

DR EVANS: No, David. There is no child. Mary was hysterical when she said she bore your child. Why, you do not know her and she is a virgin.

SCOTT: Was I not born of a virgin?

DR EVANS: Well, now, yes, of course…

SCOTT: But it is not for *that* child he comes …

DR SAMUELS: Enough! Stop this! I cannot take any more. Send him away …

DR EVANS: My dear Susan, of course, of course, do not stress yourself. I will send for someone at once. *(He makes a call)* This is Dr Evans. We need a male orderly at the Psychiatric Wing at once. What? This is ridiculous. Well, as soon as you can. There will be someone along shortly.

DR SAMUELS: Thank you. Thank you. I don't know what came over me.

DR EVANS: Perfectly understandable in your condition. Now sit here and relax.

SCOTT: Ah!

DR SAMUELS: What is he staring at?

SCOTT: Can't you see him? There he is.

DR EVANS: Please, sit and be quiet David.

SCOTT: They seek to gather grapes of thorns. The vine they pass by.

DR EVANS: Would you like a glass of water?

DR SAMUELS: No, thanks but could you try and get hold of Doug and get him to come and fetch me?

DR EVANS: Of course, of course. Do you have a number? I knew you shouldn't have come in today.

DR SAMUELS: Perhaps you were right. It's there in my handbag. Oh!

DR EVANS: Susan. What is it?

SCOTT: He is still standing there. He has stood there the whole time. It is she he is waiting for. Look there! Now he is going to her. Doctor, give me your trust. I have not the power to stop him until you do.

DR SAMUELS: Bit of a pain. Had it before but not so …Oh! *(She collapses in pain, clutching her chest)*

SCOTT: Listen – that is the scythe … He cut wrong, the stroke went astray.

DR EVANS: Susan! *(He catches her as she faints and puts her on the desk, taking his coat for a pillow. Goes to phone)* This is Dr Evans on the Psychiatric Wing. I want a crash team here now…now! It's Dr Samuels. *(He tries resuscitation but finally gives up. Goes to phone)* Dr Evans here. Stand down the crash team but I will need a doctor here as soon as possible. Yes, yes but there is still a chance for the baby but it has to be now! What? No, I can't induce labour. I haven't the equipment here and I haven't practised medicine in years. Send someone now! *(Goes to Dr Samuels)* Oh God I can feel the baby struggling for life. Where are they?

SCOTT: This time the scythe has cut true. Dazzling white! Stop will you!

DR EVANS: Please, David. Be quiet. She and the baby are dead.

SCOTT: Stop! – I tell you. In my Father's name I command you: give them here, give me back the souls – you *shall!* …You refuse? Then go – I shall meet you again. When the hour of faith has come, you shall bring them back.

DR EVANS: Where is that doctor?

MARY: *(Coming round)* Doctor? Yes a doctor. Get her a doctor.

67

DR EVANS: Mary. Let me look at you. You have had a shock. You are in hospital. I am Dr Evans.

MARY: Why am I in hospital? Aren't I O.K.?

DR EVANS: You seem to be fine now but we were all worried about you. Can you stand? I need to get you back to your ward as soon as possible. Your mother and father will be here soon to take you home.

MARY: *(Seeing David)* Is he all right. He looks all right. I am sorry about the girl you were with. She just stepped out in front of us, there was nothing Si could do. He did the right thing and waited for the police but I just ran off home and went straight to my room. It was wrong of me but my head was spinning; I kept just seeing her face as we hit her; she opened her mouth as if to say something but couldn't speak, couldn't speak. I couldn't speak.

SCOTT: But the power of your faith has cured you.

MARY: What's he saying?

DR EVANS: David, Mr Scott, had a bad shock too and he hasn't quite come to himself yet.

SCOTT: You believed in me and touched the hem of my garment and the devil that was in you was driven out.

MARY: I don't understand, what devil?

DR EVANS: Mr Scott is still a little confused about who he is but we are all working to make him well again.

MARY: Is it true that he cured me, made me better?

DR EVANS: Well, you seemed to have a sudden convulsion when you took hold of Mr Scott and that appears to have brought you round.

MARY: *(going to David)* Thank you.

DR EVANS: Thank me not but thank my father in heaven who gave me the power to cast out the devil that plagued you.

MARY: I am not sure what you mean but after what we did to you … It was very kind. Your girlfriend …

DR EVANS: Sarah.

MARY: Sarah. Is she … is she *(she sees Dr Samuels and screams. David takes her in his arms)*. Is that her? Why is she here?

DR EVANS: No, no, that is my colleague, Dr Samuels, she has fainted. We are just waiting for another doctor to come and look at her.

MARY: She is dead, I know it.

SCOTT: She is not dead; she is asleep.

MARY: Do you believe that David?

DR EVANS: David – please!

SCOTT: The Lord giveth, the Lord taketh away.

MARY: When I was not myself, when my mind was somewhere else, when I was in deep despair, I knew my body was slipping away that I would soon die in a sea of darkness. And then I heard your voice. You said that your love was greater than my weariness, your faith stronger than my insight. That you had prayed to your Father and was allowed to visit this tottering world once more. And I believed and wanted to come to you and but the devil took hold of me again and I was to tempt you with the body of Sarah, to test you once more like the Devil had tested you in the desert.

SCOTT: Sarah! *(Falls to his knees)*

MARY: No, no David I am not Sarah. I am Mary.

DR EVANS: *(He has been standing by Dr Samuels)* Man proposes, but – ah look at her. When I think of the day she told me she was pregnant. The smile on her face as she handed me a coffee.

MARY: There must be a purpose in this, Doctor, or it wouldn't have happened.

DR EVANS: You think so. And what purpose would that be?

MARY: There is beauty even in sorrow. Life even in death.

DR EVANS: Oh, the life everlasting, the resurrection of the flesh when the trumpet sounds.

MARY: Yes.

DR EVANS: "Oh death, where is they sting? O grave, where is thy victory?"
Well, I have seen too much of death to know that it is final and if you can see any
point in the death of a beautiful woman and her child, then I can't. No point at all.
I must get her moved and phone her husband.

SCOTT: *(His voice changes. He speaks normally)*. No, do not move her. Our sore
grief and bitter loss are really only proofs of God's love.

DR EVANS: David? David Scott? Have you come back?

SCOTT: Yes, Dr Evans, I've come back.

DR EVANS: Dr Evans? Did you say 'Dr Evans'? David! Your eyes! You're all
right again then?

SCOTT: Yes, I'm – all right, as you call it.

DR EVANS: The death of your fiancé had given you a shock, caused a breakdown
and delusions but you seem to have recovered your senses. And you memory as
well?

SCOTT: It has all come back; gradually. I had to have peace and solitude – to
collect my thoughts – thousands of them.

DR EVANS: Well, well. And here you are – here you are – in your right mind.

SCOTT: No, not mine but yours. My mind has become like yours – all of you. I've
returned to fear; grown wise with your wisdom. As for these senses that I have
recovered – can I use them more wisely than to pray to God to take them away
again? Where is the sure and certain hope of resurrection?

DR EVANS: David, David, we are just poor mortals …

SCOTT: That is despair if you like. Here we all stand, as defenceless in the face of
death as naked nestlings in the cat's-claw of fate. You cling to your flimsy
heathenish conjectures and your home-made human consolations. And yet it was
for you that Christ lived, died and rose again; to you that he brought the Word, as
Prometheus once brought fire.

DR EVANS: Now then David …

SCOTT: I know it is difficult. But if you hadn't enough Christian blood in you to count on the triumph of Easter, you might at least have the courage of prayer and have asked Him whether you might have her back. That hasn't occurred to you at all?

DR EVANS: You said yourself, 'Thou shalt not tempt the Lord thy God'.

SCOTT: *(Agitated and shouting)* That's why you could have asked whether you might. Look – I have asked. I have returned to myself and was strong and full of expectation; and here I stand with my spirits stunned by your grief and doubting – yes and resignation, frozen powerless like myself.

DR EVANS: What can be the use of standing and shouting across this poor woman's dead body?

SCOTT: Because, my dear Doctor, you honest consistent man, who never insulted God by pretending to believe in Him – because it's so pitiable that, while God is good and all-powerful, His earth should yet lie sprawling in wretchedness just because among His believers there isn't one who believes. Is there really nobody? Not a single one of you to support me, while I pray for a miracle to come down to us? I tell you – all things are possible for him that believeth.

DR EVANS: You mustn't overstrain your nerves, David.

SCOTT: Dr Samuels, must you lie and rot, because the times are rotten? Well then – let it be! Take her away. Go on with your half-beliefs and shift for yourselves! And let me return to the darkness – to the merciful gloom of the night. *(His fire seems to die down. Dully -)* Look, there it comes already.

MARY: *(quietly slipping her hand into his)* Come on David, be quick.

SCOTT: *(rekindling)* The child! The greatest in the kingdom of heaven! I forgot *you.* Yes, yes – salvation is with the child … *(to Mary)* Now then, look at this woman. When I call on the name of Jesus, she will rise up. Now look at her child. And, next, I shall command you, you dead –

DR EVANS: David, that's enough, let me have you taken away …

SCOTT: Will you unwittingly do Satan's errand in the guise of reason! You're crippling his power. You have always persecuted prophets and stoned apostles. Away with you!

DR EVANS: I'll not move. I have my responsibilities as your doctor.

SCOTT: Very well, then. Stay here.   *(He prays)* Hear me, O Father above. Give me the Word – the Word that Christ brought down to us from heaven – the creative, quickening Word of life. Give it me *now! (A pause)* Hear me, you that are dead. In the name of Jesus, who overthrew the grave – if God will, come back to life! I say to you – woman arise.
(Dr Samuels opens her eyes, with a slight movement of her head.)

DR EVANS: Susan!

MARY: God almighty!

DR SAMUELS: The child – where is it? Is it alive?

MARY: Yes, it's at home with God; but you are living with us – with us – with us.

DR EVANS: This is a physical impossibility. It just can't happen. But I said I wasn't a medical doctor. David are you …

SCOTT: No, I am only a little tired. No, my dear doctor, life is just beginning for us.

MARY: Oh, David – life, life!

DR EVANS: Life!

END

GEORGE FOX AND MARGARET FELL GET STUCK IN A LIFT

A Play in One Act
by
Alan Avery

Characters:

ANNOUNCER: A middle-aged man
SIR RUPERT ETHERINGTON: A middle-aged man
MARGARET FELL: A middle-aged woman
GEORGE FOX: A middle-aged soldier

This play was first performed at Pickering Quaker Meeting House on 1st October 2011 with the following cast:

ANNOUNCER: Alan Avery
SIR RUPERT ETHERINGTON: Alan Avery
MARGARET FELL: Martina McClements
GEORGE FOX: Alan Avery

GEORGE FOX AND MARGARET FELL GET STUCK IN A LIFT

(A dark stage. On the desk a console, a telephone and an in-tray on top of which is the Green Party Manifesto. Over the speakers comes the sound of a crowd chanting 'Maggy, Maggy' and then cheering)

ANNOUNCER: Incredible scenes here outside Downing Street as Margaret Fell, leader of the Green Party, leaves Buckingham Palace, heading for Downing Street as Prime Minister of the United Kingdom. Who would have thought it? The election seemed a close race between the Labour and Conservative Parties and yet, this almost unknown housewife from Harrogate has swept to power. And yes, here she is, entering Downing Street, stepping out of her car *(cheers)* and with a nervous wave, entering Downing Street for the first time. *(cheers "Maggy, Maggy"). Enter MARGARET FELL a middle-aged woman. She enters slowly, in a daze and sits behind the desk staring blankly before her. Enter SIR RUPERT ETHERINGTON)*

SIR RUPERT: Good afternoon Prime Minister. And may I, on behalf of the Civil Service and all your staff here at Downing Street, offer my sincere congratulations.

MARGARET: Who ... ?

SIR RUPERT: Who am I? Of course, we have never met before, excuse me. Sir Rupert Etherington, Cabinet Secretary. Head of the Civil Service. Your right hand man - literally, I will be sitting by your right hand in Cabinet Meetings to offer advice and make sure things you decide get done.

MARGARET: How did I ... ?

SIR RUPERT: How did you become Prime Minister? I have to admit it came as a real surprise to us all here - but a very welcome one I assure you. A breath of fresh air, so to speak.

MARGARET: But I ...

SIR RUPERT: It is tricky to understand but if I could use a footballing analogy. I understand you follow football. Well, under our new proportional, deferred vote, list system, everyone got to put their candidates in order of choice. So let us say there are 600 constituencies, divided roughly between the Labour and the Conservative Parties - we can forget the Lib-Dems after the unfortunate badger in the potting shed incident. Well, all the Labour supporters in the Labour constituencies put their man as number one on the list, scoring three point, so to speak and, as you would expect, they put the Tory candidate last, nul points for them and the reverse in the Conservative constituencies. So three hundred time 3 for the Labour Party or 900 points and 300 time three for the Conservative Party, also 900 points. Now here was the thing nobody counted on. Everyone liked you. You came across as so sincere in the debates that were broadcast and what with all the climate and water and power problems we have been having, everyone thought they ought to do something, even if it was only to put you second on their ballot paper. And everyone did. So six hundred times two points is 1200 points, a clear majority for the Green Party. Congratulations, Prime Minister.

MARGARET: But the turn out ...

SIR RUPERT: Yes, very disappointing. Less than 50% and that certainly played a part in the calculations.

SONG: APATHY

MARGARET:

The votes are in
We have a winner
The entire electorate we did consult
The polls are closed
Ballots are counted
And breathlessly we wait for the result

To the sites
We'll send our pundits
To spin and make excuses and to gloss
We can announce the vote has gone in favour
Overwhelmingly of not giving a toss

SIR RUPERT AND MARGARET:

Apathy, Apathy We shrug our shoulders happily
At whatever challenges the future brings
At the bedrock of our nation is our sheer disinclination
To get worked up about a bloody thing

MARGARET:

When confronted with democracy
The British way is to ignore it

I'm not even sure this counts
Surely this cannot be quorate (look up the word quorate)

Apathy, apathy
It's part of our anatomy
Half the British people speak at last
They made their mark
They took their choice
And said with one resounding voice
That either way, they're not especially arsed.

SIR RUPERT AND MARGARET

Apathy, apathy
It's part of our anatomy
Half the British people speak at last
They made their mark
They took their choice
And said with one resounding voice
That either way, they're not especially arsed.

MARGARET: So what happens, next Sir Rupert? Where do I go from here?

SIR RUPERT: Well, before holding your first cabinet meeting, you will need to choose your Ministers. Then you can start putting into effect all the wonderful and unusual ideas you outlined in your very interesting manifesto. There will be 350 Green M.Ps. out there waiting for the phone to ring. I have taken the preliminary step of having our dossiers on all your successful candidates brought in and matched to the relevant posts, Foreign Secretary, Chancellor of the Exchequer and so on.

MARGARET: I see.

SIR RUPERT: And here is our first little problem. Although we could easily match over two hundred of your colleagues to the post of Secretary of State for Energy and the Environment - we suggest Professor Coles from Cambridge, very eminent - the other posts were more problematic. Foreign Secretary for example. We narrowed it down to John Hoskins who has an Irish wife and an up-to-date passport and for Chancellor of the Exchequer, Hillary Devenport who has a GCSE in maths and is treasurer of her local branch of 'Save the Children'. But here is the complete list for your approval.

MARGARET: It's not very ...

SIR RUPERT: Now don't worry Prime Minister. I'm sure it will all go well and I and my colleagues throughout the civil service will be here to advise and guide you. After all, politicians come and politicians go but the civil service with our years of experience and expertise goes on for ever.

MARGARET: Without all those bothersome elections to have to worry about.

SIR RUPERT: Quite so. Will that be all for the moment, Prime Minister?

MARGARET: Yes, yes, thank you.

SIR RUPERT: Well, I will leave you with the cabinet list and when you are ready we can begin to make the phone calls. Here also are your appointments for the day. I have put Field Marshall Fox first on the list. Get it over with so to speak, although I realise it must be something of an embarrassment for you. If you like I can...

MARGARET: No, no. As you say, let's get it over with.

SIR RUPERT: Very wise Prime Minister. If you need me just press number one on the console there and I will be right with you. *(Exit Sir Rupert)*

(Margaret begins to look at the list but puts it down with a sigh. She picks up the phone and dials a number)

MARGARET: Sophie? Is that you? Yes, Margaret. Yes, here in Downing Street. You saw me on the telly? How did I look, was my hair all right? No, King William was charming - he wouldn't let me kiss his hand or anything said Kate would get jealous. I know. *(giggles)*. How's life in Blackbird Avenue? Look, thanks for seeing to the cat and all that. Is she O.K.? Could you water the plants and put the bin out tomorrow? And the mail ... ? What? Seven sacks full? Oh Lord. Just leave them and I'll have a look when I get home. I don't know when. It's all a bit hectic here at the moment. I'm supposed to choose a cabinet. No not from IKEA, you know the Ministers and all that. I know, I know. How are things now between you and Simon? Oh good. I know, I know. I mean look at Richard and Davina. They have been happily married for sixteen years and yet he is still not perfect. Look you must come round here to number 10 for a cup of tea and a natter as soon as I'm settled in. The wallpaper here is horrendous; I don't know what the Milibands were thinking of. Yes, yes. Thanks again Sophie. See you soon. Bye. Let me have a look. *(She picks up the list)* Oh ... I don't know any of them. *(She ticks at random)* How many is that? Twenty. That should be enough. I can always change my mind once I get to know them. I suppose I had better read the manifesto. *(flicks through it)*. Oh dear. "We will bring in a bill to ban all nuclear power stations and patio heaters", "There will be free University Education for all, regardless of age or aptitude", "The armed forces, the armed forces ...", this was all easy when we never thought we would have to do anything about it.

VOICE OFF: The Chief of the General Staff, Field Marshall, Sir George Fox, DSCO, MBE.

(George Fox marches smartly on to the set and salutes Margaret. He then throws his hat onto her desk and drops into a chair)

GEORGE: What the fuck is going on Maggy?

MARGARET: Well, hello to you too. I don't think you should speak to your Prime Minister like that. And I don't recall asking you to sit.

GEORGE: And I don't recall saying it was all right for you to be Prime Minister but a fat lot of notice you took of that!

MARGARET: *(Whispers)* Yes, all right. But lets face it, neither of us expected this to happen.

GEORGE: No.

MARGARET: But it has. And it's a wonderful opportunity to do some good in this country and in the world and I would appreciate your cooperation and a little discretion.

GEORGE: Look, I agreed, to hold off on the divorce until after the election, on the off chance you were elected as MP for wherever it was you were standing.

MARGARET: Harrogate.

GEORGE: Wherever. But what now? 'The Prime Minister announced today she will be holding a review of Government spending and divorcing her husband of twenty-eight years standing on some spurious ground or other'. I can see that going down well in the shires.

MARGARET: What do you mean 'some spurious ground'? You make it sound as if you were the innocent party!

GEORGE: It takes two to make a divorce. I might have gone a little astray with young Florence but you can't say there was no blame on your side.

MARGARET: Blame, blame. What blame? It was you who were unfaithful with Florence and goodness knows who else.

GEORGE: There was no-one else.

MARGARET: How old was she?

GEORGE: Twenty-eight.

MARGARET: Really? She looked older. But you said yourself she was spiritual and not interested in appearances, which was fortunate for you.

GEORGE: All those nights away from home at conferences and meetings. I never saw you from one weekend to the next. The most fun we had towards the end was when we wrote our wills. And those phone calls from Andy Johnson. I don't think they were all about focus groups and policy changes were they?

MARGARET: Andy was my agent. Of course we spoke a lot together.

GEORGE: At three o'clock in the morning!

MARGARET: Well, Andy was very enthusiastic.

GEORGE: So you took the calls downstairs.

MARGARET: I was trying not to disturb you!

GEORGE: And then coming back looking all flushed and starry-eyed.

MARGARET: Andy had a great way of enthusing you.

GEORGE: Is that what they call it in political circles.

MARGARET: I will not let you shift any of the responsibility for this divorce onto me, I will not. It all comes down to your jealousy.

GEORGE: Jealousy!

MARGARET: We were fine while I was prepared to be the little housewife, holding your dinner parties and flirting with your superiors.

GEORGE: Don't tell me you didn't enjoy it and don't say we weren't happy.

MARGARET: After a fashion. But I wanted more. I wanted my own life. I wanted to achieve something more than just being Mrs George Fox.

GEORGE: Most women would have been satisfied with that. But not you. I put up with you being a Quaker, although my family was dead against it, said it would hold back my career.

MARGARET: But it didn't did it?

GEORGE: No. I have to say, I couldn't have done it without you. But then, member of the Green Party, then elected leader and going back to your maiden name so that *I* wouldn't be an embarrassment!

MARGARET: We agreed all that at the time. Why are you bringing all this up again?

SONG:

GEORGE:

I can still remember
The day I first saw you
You came walking by
And you gave me such a smile

MARGARET:

And I can still remember
When you came marching by
I stood and watched
Like a little girl
It made me cry

BOTH

Yesterday you were (I was) just a little mouse
Too timid and too shy to leave the house
Uh ah uh ah uh ah
A helpmate, that's what I (you) thought
Someone to help and support me (you)

GEORGE:

Your eyes are dark blue
I saw that suddenly
For you looked at me, a short second
When I marched by

MARGARET:

And everything stood still
In that short second
And my heart it thumped

So I thought that it would break

BOTH: Yesterday, you were just etc

MARGARET: What are you saying? That we should give it another go for old times' sake? I think events have moved on too much for that but I would be grateful if we could hold off on the divorce just a little longer until I have had a chance to settle into the job.

GEORGE: The divorce was your idea, remember. So if you want to wait that's fine by me.

MARGARET: Thank you. And let's stop pretending it was some little affair with Sophie or Andy that has pushed us apart.

GEORGE: Yes. How is our errant daughter? I haven't seen her for some time?

MARGARET: Alice is O.K. still a little shocked, about us two I mean. But she is old enough to understand.

GEORGE: Is she still going to marry that drip from the Meeting House?

MARGARET: David is not a drip. He is a very sensitive and charming boy. He is very fond of Alice. She could do a lot worse. And he still wants to marry her despite little Joe. He was at the birth you know.

GEORGE: Really. And I suppose he asked all the usual questions – is it a boy, is it a girl, is it normal, is it white? And what's he going to be when he's finished University? Don't tell me, a teacher, a social worker, a civil servant?

MARGARET: He's talking about the law or something to do with the civil rights movement or even a position with one of the big charities if he can get an interview, it's not easy these days what with all the ....

GEORGE: Mm.

MARGARET: You haven't been listening to a word I've said!

GEORGE: The law, civil rights movement, big charity.

MARGARET: That's so typical of you George, you deliberately listened out of spite.

GEORGE: Can't he get a proper job like …. Never mind.

MARGARET: You can mention his name.

GEORGE: It doesn't matter, forget it.

MARGARET: But this was an official appointment not a personal one. Was there something official you needed to discuss with me?

GEORGE: Yes, I need your authorisation for a small military action. It's in another sovereign state's waters so we can't do it without civilian authority. Normally, it would go before the cabinet but as we don't have one, Sir Rupert tells me your signature will do. Just sign here.

MARGARET: What do you mean, 'a small military action'? I know nothing of all this.

GEORGE: Of course not. We have kept it quiet, low key, for the sake of all those involved but your predecessor was kept fully briefed and was right behind us.

MARGARET: Well yes, he would be but you know our position on the use of armed force to solve diplomatic problems. I am not going to sign anything which lets you put lives at risk.

GEORGE: Are you speaking now as Prime Minister or as an airy fairy Quaker? Because you had better be clear from the start, the two don't mix. Nobody minds if you make statements and declarations and hold your nice quiet vigils as long as you go on paying your taxes and stay out of politics.

MARGARET: I can't accept that. There must be a way of solving these problems without the use of the armed services. Diplomatic, economic, the force of reason and morality.

GEORGE: Which planet are you on? These things all sound very feasible in the sanctity of the University common room or the quiet of the Meeting House. Look, I know where you are coming from and in theory everyone agrees with wanting peace. Believe me, soldiers don't like wars. They use up men and resources and these days you can never be sure if you will win. It's good there are people like you setting the standard of what mankind should be like. Looking to the future and showing us what we could become if we could only find a way of combating evil without the use of force but out there in the real world …

MARGARET: The real world, as you call it, has brought nothing but killing and misery and the spending of scarce resources on an unprecedented scale. And what do we have to show for it?

GEORGE: Democracy, the right to live as we want and not how some dictator tells us to live. Or is that too high a price for you to pay?

MARGARET: We are talking theoretically here. Just tell me the situation and I will have a clearer grasp of what is going on.

GEORGE: *The Star of India*. You have been following the news?

MARGARET: Remind me.

GEORGE: *The Star of India* is a British oil tanker currently being held by Somali pirates who want ten million pounds for the release of the ship and its crew of thirty.

MARGARET: Yes, yes. So why don't we just pay? We can still just about afford it I suppose and the ship and cargo must be worth twenty times that amount.

GEORGE: Because, let me remind you, the British Government does not give in to blackmail. If we pay this ransom, it will be open house on every British ship from Kuwait to the Isle of White ferry. We have entered into international agreements on this very subject.

MARGARET: So let's wait, sit it out, see what happens. Negotiate.

GEORGE: Appeal to their better nature.

MARGARET: There is that of God in everyone.

GEORGE: Not this lot. They'd slit your throat for a pack of cigarettes. Anyway, things have taken a turn for the worse.

MARGARET: How?

GEORGE: They have said that unless we pay up by nine o'clock tonight, our time, in three hours, they will begin to kill a member of the crew every hour until we do.

MARGARET: Do you believe them?

GEORGE: Oh, yes. We know this lot of old. Believe me they will. But don't worry we have the matter in hand.

MARGARET: How?

GEORGE: We had wind that something like this would happen when *The Star* left the Gulf. MI5 seem to have got it right for once. So I have four SAS troopers embedded with the crew. They are fully armed and just need the word to take on the pirates. There are only ten of them and if we send two more men with the ransom, the odds look good, what with surprise and our superior training and weaponry.

MARGARET: But lives will be lost?

GEORGE: I bloody well hope so. Ten of them and every one a Somali.

MARGARET: Then I can't authorise the action. I will not put my name to a paper that will send ten men, maybe more to their deaths. There must be another way.

GEORGE: Yes, of course, I was forgetting. Let's all pray or have a special meeting for worship to strengthen our faith that the good Lord will send down the light to these poor men, let them see the error of their ways and surrender meekly. Is that what you had in mind?

MARGARET: Do not underestimate the power of prayer.

GEORGE: And don't you underestimate the evil of these men. If you don't know their record then look it up. Hundreds killed, men women and children. Some after the ransom was paid so that the pirates couldn't be identified. Women raped and mutilated to encourage relatives and governments to pay up. You don't negotiate with these people. Or if you do, you are a more naïve than I thought you were.

MARGARET: Let me look at the other options before I go down your military road.

GEORGE: Yes, of course. But I suggest we go to the war room where all the information is coming in and you can see the situation for yourself. We have a Somali interpreter so if we get a chance, you can talk to the pirates and work your charm on them but don't be surprised if they don't have the first idea who you are.

MARGARET: I see. Yes, if it is possible, I want to speak to them. Where is this war room?

GEORGE: Over the road at the Ministry of Defence. There is a direct link, an underground corridor from Number 10 to the Ministry.

MARGARET: I didn't know that.

GEORGE: You weren't supposed to. I had better tell Sir Rupert what is going on. *(Goes to console on desk)*. Rupert, it's George. I'm taking the PM over to the war room to brief her on *The Star of India* situation. Yes, that's right. We'll take the lift. Mind the shop will you? Come on. This way.

(George and Margaret enter the lift. George presses a button)

Going down.

MARGARET: Ladies underwear and ironmongery.

(The lift judders to a halt)

GEORGE: What the hell is going on now?

MARGARET: We seem to have come to a halt.

GEORGE: That's all I need.

MARGARET: Is there an emergency phone?

GEORGE: Those things hadn't been invented when this lift was installed.

MARGARET: Here try my mobile. There's a good signal. *(She gives George her mobile)*.

GEORGE: Yes, right. Don't worry I'll soon get us out of here. Hello, put me through to Sir Rupert. Field Marshall Fox. Yes, you blithering idiot get on with it! Rupert? George. The PM and I are stuck in the lift from No 10 to the corridor. Lucky the PM had a mobile. Very amusing. Just get us out of here will you? All right. Someone will be along in a minute.

MARGARET: Good. I've never liked being in these small spaces.

GEORGE: I remember when you panicked on the ghost train in Brighton.

MARGARET: That was a long time ago. You were just a captain then. Fancy you remembering.

GEORGE: How could I forget? You got out of the train and ran back to the entrance, screaming all the way. You scared the life out of the man dressed as a skeleton. I had to pay him £10 to keep quiet.

MARGARET: Daniel was conceived in Brighton, you know. That night, back at the hotel, probably.

GEORGE: Was he? I didn't know. What's taking them so long?

MARGARET: You still wont talk about him will you?

GEORGE: What good will it do? You will never forgive me, never forget.

MARGARET: George, I don't blame you for Dan's death, anymore than I blame myself.

GEORGE: You say that now. At the time you stopped speaking to me the day we got the news from Afghanistan. You blamed me all right. It was me who encouraged him to join up, I know. Left to himself, he would probably have been a teacher or a civil servant.

MARGARET: I didn't know who to blame. You were the nearest target. Yes, I suppose I blamed you for wanting him to follow in your footsteps. But he was a strong enough character to know his own mind. If he hadn't wanted to be a soldier, he wouldn't have done it, not even to please you.

GEORGE: But the love went out of your eyes …*(The lift gives a sudden lurch. Margaret screams and throws her arms around George. They nearly kiss. In a graceful movement, George takes off his jacket and puts it around Margaret and then sinks to the floor in a sleep).*

MARGARET: Ever the soldier. Sleep when you can, eat when you can.

SONG 3. BLACKBIRD AVENUE

MARGARET:

Can it be true
That I still love you?
Shall we live again
In Blackbird Avenue?

For it was there

We met for the first time
One summer morning
When the birds all sang.

Four grandchildren
Or maybe just the one
Dear God,
Who decides what's to be done?

And the kitchen
You had it painted blue
Because you said
'Blue, really suites you'.

Can it be true
That I still love you?
Shall we live again
In Blackbird Avenue?
Let's try again
This time we'll make it work
We'll hold hands
In the dark

And if you say
You still love me
I'll give all this up
And set us both free.

Can it be true
That I still love you?
Shall we live again
In Blackbird Avenue?

GEORGE: What time is it? Just two hours to the deadline. Where the hell are they? *(Phones again)*. Rupert, what's going on, why are we still in here? What? I see. Well as soon as you can. Look is there any way you can patch the war room through to this phone? The PM wants to speak to the pirates if they will listen. All right do your best.

MARGARET: Problems?

GEORGE: The war room and the corridor and this lift are bomb proofed.

MARGARET: Hurray! And?

GEORGE: It means we are encased in five feet of reinforced concrete and they have to cut through that before they can get to us. Could take at least another hour. But you heard what I said about the phone?

MARGARET: Yes.

GEORGE: And if we can get through, what are you going to say to them? Be good boys and let the nice white people go.

MARGARET: I am not as naïve as you make out George. I know the chances of my persuading them to do the right thing are very small but I have to try.

GEORGE: And if you don't succeed, you will let my men take them on?

MARGARET: Don't make me promise that George. This is the first test of my time as Prime Minister. If I behave like all the rest of them, then there will be no going back for the next five years. I have to try and break the circle of evil, the circle of violence. We have to try and do things differently or we just go on sacrificing young men like Daniel for ever.

GEORGE: Dan was a soldier. He knew the risks. It went with the job.

MARGARET: He was our only son and now he is dead. He died on some dusty plain where he and his friends had no business being for a cause which nobody believed in or even understood.

GEORGE: He was a man doing his duty, serving his government and his people. Making sure the country he was defending had a right to choose the type of government they wanted and not one forced on them by a bunch of fanatics, who, may I remind you, tried to down one of our civilian aircraft with a missile bought with money donated to set up a fresh water system.

MARGARET: Did you really have an affair with Florence?

GEORGE: I kissed her once at the office party.

MARGARET: Nothing else?

GEORGE: No.

MARGARET: Oh George, it makes me so sad … that you are such a terrible liar.

GEORGE: Yes all right. So it may have been more than a kiss. It's nothing to be ashamed of.

MARGARET: Oh yes it is. But I didn't really believe it. Florence was very sophisticated whereas your taste in women always leant more towards the sluttish.

GEORGE: And what about you and Andy?

MARGARET: What about us?

GEORGE: Don't tell me there was nothing between you.

MARGARET: He groped me once at the Party Conference.

GEORGE: I hope you slapped his face!

MARGARET: No. I rather enjoyed it. I haven't been groped in years.

GEORGE: And then what?

MARGARET: What?

GEORGE: After the grope.

MARGARET: Well, he kept trying it on. I was very flattered really.

GEORGE: But..?

MARGARET: But nothing else happened George. I told him, if he couldn't keep his hands to himself I would have to sack him as my agent and tell you. Anyway, he's a Christian, with a small c.

GEORGE: He's something beginning with a c. So why didn't you tell me?

MARGARET: And what would you have done if I had?

GEORGE: Broken his bloody neck.

MARGARET: And that's why I didn't tell you.

GEORGE: Hm.

MARGARET: Can you hear anything? Any drilling?

GEORGE: No.

MARGARET: Shouldn't we be able to hear something by now?

GEORGE: Probably. Do you want a cigarette?

MARGARET: Haven't you given up smoking yet?

GEORGE: No, I'm no quitter.

MARGARET: Not in here George, I'll suffocate.

GEORGE: Did you fall for Andy because I wasn't romantic?

MARGARET? What?

GEORGE: You know, romantic. All that luvy duvy stuff.

MARGARET: Oh, George, you are every bit as romantic as Andy, you pillock.

GEORGE: Even when I never noticed if you had had your hair done, or were wearing a new dress ...

MARGARET: Or had new shoes on.

GEORGE: You had so many.

MARGARET: My Achilles high heels. If you had started noticing, I would have been worried – concerned you were up to something. Why can't I hear any drilling or hammering George?

GEORGE: No idea. Let me try Sir Rupert again. *(He phones)* Rupert, what the hell is going on? I see. What? O.K. I'll pass her over. The shaft is so narrow only one man can work at a time and they are concerned about dropping half a ton of concrete on our heads. But they have patched us through to one of the pirates on the boat if you still want to speak to him. He speaks English by the way.

MARGARET: Yes, of course. Give me the phone. Hello, hello. Who am I speaking to? Yussaf, hello. My name is Margaret Fell. I am the British Prime Minister. No, not Thatcher, Fell. Yes that's right. Well, it's only just happened, so perhaps you haven't heard. Look, I understand you want ten million pounds to release the boat and the crew but it's very difficult for me to authorise the payment...It's really not that easy....yes, yes, I am the Prime Minister but that doesn't mean I can just hand over the money. No, I don't have ten million myself. If I did I would give it to you. Is there anything else you would accept instead of the money? Well I don't know. I am sure we could think of something. The village you live in. I could arrange for a school to be built and a fresh water supply and a clinic ... What? Your village was burned down by the Government and you had to flee. I see. I'm sorry. How old are you Yussaf? Really? The same age my son would have been. No, no. He was killed in Afghanistan. I can't even try and understand what made you into a pirate, made you want to hijack ships and threaten people – yes I understand about the threat to kill the crew members if we don't pay but as I said, it's not so easy for me right now. I know, I know. I am sure you will carry out your threat but I am trying to find a way out of this which does not involve killing or violence so please help me. I understand you will release the crew and ship once the ten million pounds is paid but you know we, the British Government, we have always said we will not give in to blackmail. Did you know this? We did pay? When? Just a moment Yussaf, don't go away. *(To George)* He says we did pay half a million pounds to have an old couple and their yacht released.

GEORGE: That was the family and friends who paid, not the government.

MARGARET: I see. *(To Yussaf)* Yussaf, that was the family and friends who paid. It was a private arrangement, not the government. Yes, I suppose so. Let me find out and get back to you but promise me you wont hurt anyone until I phone you again. Less than two hours to go. Yes. Yes. Promise me Yussaf. Yusaff. He rang off.

GEORGE: Any joy?

MARGARET: Is there no way we could make this a private arrangement, so that the government are not involved. Couldn't the shipping line pay up?

GEORGE: They want to, believe me, but the international agreements are that no payment is to be made by the owners. And don't expect the crew members' families to find ten million pounds in two hours.

MARGARET: Couldn't we find the money and give it to the families and then let them pay, so it looks like they have paid?

GEORGE: You mean tell lies? The press would be on to that like a shot. Seamen's families tend not to have millions of pounds stuffed down the sofa or friendly bank managers willing to loan them the money, however worthy the cause.

MARGARET: Think of something George. Time is running out.

GEORGE: I have given you my option. It has a good chance of succeeding. You only have to give the word.

MARGARET: George, I can't. It would make a mockery of everything I believe in, everything I have said for the last twenty years. Violence can't be the answer.

GEORGE: Who is going to make the phone call?

MARGARET: What?

GEORGE: The call to the family of the first sailor they shoot and toss his body over the side. Because they will. What are you going to say? Terribly sorry about your son Mrs Jones but you see I had a principle to uphold, one I thought it worth your son dying for.

MARGARET: It's horrible when you put it like that.

GEORGE: How else can I put it?

MARGARET: I don't know. A third party!

GEORGE: What?

MARGARET: A third party. Couldn't we get some other international agency involved? The Red Cross? The UN? Get them to pay on the understanding we would pay it back to them?

GEORGE: Same problem as before. The press and opposition would want to know why they paid and where the money came from. You would either have to stand up in the House of Commons and lie through your teeth or admit we did a deal through the back door and broke all our agreements and long-standing policies. A fine start to your premiership.

MARGARET: But I can change all the agreements and policies once I am in fully in power?

GEORGE: With your majority you could do what the hell you want and no doubt your sandal wearing, Guardian reading MPs would back you all the way. But that's in the future. Now we have to play by the present rules and solve this little problem now not in three weeks' time.

MARGARET: But I could order Sir Rupert to make arrangements for the payment if I wanted to?

GEORGE: Theoretically.

MARGARET: Why theoretically?

GEORGE: Do you think it is that easy to spirit up a bag containing ten million pounds in the middle of nowhere and get it out to the ship?

MARGARET: The pirates must know this.

GEORGE: Who knows what they know. Why not ask your friend Yussaf?

MARGARET: Very well. Get him on the phone again will you?

GEORGE: You are sure you know what you're doing?

MARGARET: No but I have to try.

GEORGE: Rupert, George again. Can you get me through to our friend Yussaf or better still tell me how they expected us to find ten million in three hours and get it to them. I see. No, hold the call to Somalia. It seems they have a numbered account in Switzerland. We can make a wire transfer. Thanks Rupert. 'Greengage' Rupert.

MARGARET: That means you wont be able to land any more men on the ship.

GEORGE: We'll find some pretext – checking everyone is all right before we pay the money.

MARGARET: Then I am going to order Sir Rupert to make the payment and hang the consequences. I'll brazen it out somehow. Give me my phone.

GEORGE: Can't do that Maggy.

MARGARET: What? George give me the phone!

GEORGE: No.

MARGARET: George, as your Prime Minister, I am ordering you to give me the bloody phone.

GEORGE: And as your Chief of Staff and husband I am telling you I can't do it.

MARGARET: *(Makes a lunge for the phone)*. Give it to me. *(They struggle but it ends with George restraining Margaret in an arm lock.)* George you are hurting me. Let go.

GEORGE: Only if you calm down. No more rough stuff Mrs Pacifist.

MARGARET: Very well. *(He releases her)*. Bastard!

GEORGE: Love you too.

MARGARET: What's going on George?

GEORGE: You just have to sit and wait and things will take their course and you will come out smelling of roses.

MARGARET: What did you mean when you said 'Greengage' to Sir Rupert and why can't I hear any banging or drilling? ... George? Answer me.

GEORGE: Figure it out for yourself Maggy.

MARGARET: This lift isn't stuck at all is it? Well?

GEORGE: No.

MARGARET: You could get us out anytime you wanted just by making a phone call to Sir Rupert. Is he in on this? 'Greengage' was a code, a password wasn't it? A password for what?

GEORGE: That you had weakened, as we thought you might and were going to cave in and that the military operation was to go ahead.

MARGARET: George, no! You can't do this. There is still a chance to resolve this peacefully. I am still in charge, your boss. I order you to cancel the operation ... George. This will be the end for you. Once I am out of here, I will have you arrested for treason or something. You could go to jail.

GEORGE: That's up to you. But I will be able to look the crew's family in the eye and tell them I did everything possible to save their lives.

MARGARET: Just let me speak to Yussaf one more time. Please George. If we can solve this without bloodshed we must at least try.

GEORGE: And what are you going to say to him? Don't promise to pay the money because it wont happen, Sir Rupert will see to that and if they don't get paid when the deadline runs out they will start killing the crew and my men have orders to take action once that starts. So what are you going to say to Yussaf?

MARGARET: I don't know George. Give me a moment. *(There follows a minute's uncomfortable silence)*. Can you get Yussaf on the phone for me George?

GEORGE: Only if you promise not to say you are going to pay the money, because you can't and don't make any other promises you can't keep because they will only take that out on the crew.

MARGARET: I understand. Yes, O.K.

GEORGE: *(on the phone)* Rupert, George. The P.M. knows the situation now about Operation Greengage but she wants to speak to the pirates again. Yes, she has promised not to say we will pay the ransom. Can you put her through again? Thanks. He's on the line.

MARGARET: Yusaff. It's me again. Margaret Fell. The British Prime Minister. No, I cannot get you the money. Don't ring off Yusaff, let me speak. Yusaff, what you are doing is wrong, you must know that. In my religion and I am sure in your religion, killing innocent people is wrong. I can't begin to understand the conditions you and your friends live in and what has made you take up this life of crime but you know what you are doing is evil and will only bring you sorrow and unhappiness. If you let the crew and the ship go I promise you that I will take a personal interest in your country and do everything I can to help it. We can send doctors and teachers and food and help to build up your country so that the young people can be educated and find jobs instead of turning to crime like you. Think in the long term Yusaff, think of your country and your people instead of just your own immediate wants and greed …..I know we should have done all this a long time ago instead of now when there is a threat to our people but I have only just become Prime Minister and I want to start right now doing the decent thing. You will talk to your friends? That's wonderful Yusaff. Yes, I will stay on the phone….Oh George, it looks as though they might leave the ship peacefully.

GEORGE: It's a long shot but let's hope so. Don't get your hopes up.

MARGARET: What did I tell you, George, there is that of God in everyone. It's just a matter of appealing to better nature and giving alternatives to the wrong course of action. Wait, he's back ………I see, … I see… Yusaff, you and your friends must get off the ship … there are soldiers on board with orders to kill you.. you must….

95

GEORGE: No! No you stupid, … *(George wrestles with Margaret for the phone which she refuses to give up. George punches her hard twice in the face, knocking her unconscious and then takes the phone).* Rupert they know about my men on board … never mind … give the order for action now before it's too late. Yes, my authority. And open the bloody doors. *(George picks up Margaret and carries her back into the office. He sits her on a chair and then throws water in her face).*

MARGARET: *(Coming round)* What hit me?

GEORGE: I did.

MARGARET: I can't believe it.

GEORGE: If you had been a man, I would have killed you.

MARGARET: George!

GEORGE: What the hell were you thinking of? To blow my men's cover like that! If any of them have been harmed, I will hold you personally responsible.

MARGARET: I did the right thing.

GEORGE: You think so. What did Yusaff say to you?

MARGARET: It doesn't matter.

GEORGE: Of course it matters. Tell me!

MARGARET: He spoke to his friends and they laughed at him. Said they would kill him first instead of the crew member and throw him overboard. Said he was a traitor for talking to a dog of a politician and a woman at that. I just couldn't think of anything happening to that young man, I had to get him off the ship …Did you and Sir Rupert think up this whole elaborate ruse? How dare you!

GEORGE: Believe it or not, we were thinking of you.

MARGARET: Me?

GEORGE: I was sure you wouldn't sign the release for the military action and Sir Rupert had his doubts. You winning the election was not part of our planning. We had a couple of hours to think of some way of rescuing the crew and yet not involving you. So we came up with the lift solution. If you didn't sign, I was to hold you in the lift until it was all over and then you could legitimately say that the

96

military action went ahead without your approval and in the future we would do things differently. If it has been a success then no long term harm done.

MARGARET: If it has been a failure?

GEORGE: We'll cross that bridge when we get to it.

MARGARET: How soon will we know?

GEORGE: Soon.

MARGARET: What did you mean when you said you would hold me personally responsible?

GEORGE: If any of my men or the crew are killed or harmed as a direct result of your interference, I will let the world know why. It'll be the end of me and the end of your political career. Think yourself lucky if you are not impeached and charged with treason. Still, with your majority, you will probably just about get away with just resigning. But if I were you, I would leave the country before someone takes a shot at you.

MARGARET: Will you come with me George? *(The phone rings)*.

GEORGE: That'll be Sir Rupert from the war room. *(He takes the phone)*. Yes,... yes, she's here. I'll tell her. Will you hold the press conference? No, I wont be there. I don't know, I'll ask her.

MARGARET: Well?

GEORGE: Eight pirates killed, two captured, including your friend Yusaff who gave himself up. All the crew O.K. One of my men killed, the others are fine. The ship is on its way to South Africa.

MARGARET: I'm sorry. About your soldier.

GEORGE: He knew the risk. We'll look after his family.

MARGARET: What did Sir Rupert want you to ask me?

GEORGE: The press conference. Will you attend? Can we agree a common line, a consistent story?

MARGARET: Do you still hold me responsible for your man's death?

GEORGE: I can't be sure. It could well have happened anyway. I'll wait till I get a full report from the unit commander.

MARGARET: If I attend this conference and say that although I am pleased about the outcome, I did not approve of the action, the use of violence, to solve this dispute, and in the future we will do things differently, do you think people will understand?

GEORGE: Possibly. You will face some tough questioning from the press and the opposition. Can you take it?

MARGARET: I don't' know but I can't give up now we have just begun.

GEORGE: And what happens next time, next time there is a situation when all else has failed and the military option is on the table? Will you run and hide in the lift until someone else sorts it out?

MARGARET: I can't make big decisions like that on the spur of the moment. We need to get everyone together, talk it through so that we can come up with a foreign policy that means we don't have to even consider the use of the armed services.

GEORGE: The very best of luck because as soon as the enemies of this country realise we are not prepared to fight to defend what we believe in, we will be ignored, mocked and trodden on at will. Is that what you want?

MARGARET: I want this country to be seen as the first to at least try to conduct ourselves on the basis of trust, mutual respect and one who tries to solve its problems and difficulties through negotiation, compromise, discussion. We have to look for outcomes which are mutually beneficial rather than ones in which we win and someone else loses.

GEORGE: 'I have in my hand a piece of paper'. The very best of luck. I'm sorry I wont be around to see how you get on.

MARGARET: George, don't walk out on me. Stay and help me.

GEORGE: If this is the way you are going – and don't get me wrong, I wish you luck and I hope it all works – but if this is the way you are going then there is no place for an honest soldier like me and I don't see where you are going to find one who will operate in the way you want. What are the armed services to become? Oxfam in uniform? And what about the nuclear forces?

MARGARET: I know George. I might be taking on more than I can cope with. Stay and help me, advise me.

GEORGE: I'll be around until you find a suitable replacement at least. I wont leave you entirely in the hands of Sir Rupert. Trust him. He has your best interests at heart. I think he might even actually believe in some of the stuff you've been peddling. He was a hippy way back in the 1960s believe it or not.

MARGARET: Yes, you should hear him on the bongos.

GEORGE: What?

MARGARET: Never mind. What about us?

GEORGE: I can't say Maggie. You started that ball rolling so I'll leave it with you.

MARGARET: What will you do, if you leave the army, resign I mean?

GEORGE: I haven't thought that far ahead. Who knows? Maybe some voluntary work.

MARGARET: Not Somalia.

GEORGE: No, not Somalia. Well, if there is nothing else I will leave the country in your capable hands. *(He salutes, and leaves)*.

MARGARET: George! *(She sits behind her desk, head in hands and begins to cry)*. This wont do. *(Presses console)*. Sir Rupert, would you come in, we need to discuss the press conference and I think you have some explaining to do, or am I looking for a new chief secretary to the cabinet? *(Takes a deep breath and begins to look through the papers on her desk as the lights fade)*.

END

ONE OF THAT DESPISED PEOPLE

A Play in One Act
by
Alan Avery

Additional dialogue by Anthony Avery and Joanna Bond

Characters:

MAJOR BROOKES: A middle-aged man
FREYA JACKSON: A woman in her thirties

This play was first performed at Pickering Quaker Meeting House on 29th
September 2012 with the following cast:

MAJOR BROOKES: Alan Avery
FREYA JACKSON: Joanna Bond

ONE OF THAT DESPISED PEOPLE

(The opening chorus of 'The Mikado' play, interspersed with the following radio style announcements:

If you want to know who we are,
We are gentlemen of Japan:
On many a vase and jar,
On many a screen and fan, *(The leader appeared in front of a cheering crown in York and promised a swift end to this war with complete victory over the Mercians)*

We figure in lively paint:
Out attitude's queer and quaint
You're wrong if you think it ain't, oh! *(Fresh riots have broken out between Jews and Christians in Sunderland which had to be put down by the army)*

If you think we are worked by strings
Like a Japanese marionette,
You don't understand these things:
It is simply Court etiquette. *(Mercian gunboats shelled Bridlington today. 15 civilians were killed. The leader has promised swift revenge with attacks on Mercian seaside towns)*

Perhaps you suppose this throng
Can't keep it up all day long?
If that's your idea, you're wrong, oh! *(The petrol and water rations have been cut by a further 20% All are urged not to travel unless really necessary)*

If that's your idea, you're wrong.
If you want to know who we are,
We are gentlemen of Japan:
On vase and jar on screen and fan.
On many a jar, oh *(gunfire, aircraft noise)*
On vase and jar on screen and fan.

Major Brookes enters. He wears a greatcoat and surgical mask, which he does not take off. He carries a briefcase. He switches on the heater which he taps but it does not work. He tries the electric kettle but again with no result. He takes off his mask and sniffs the air. He sits at his desk and begins to examine a file, playing with the paper-weight. A knock)

MAJOR BROOKES: Yes!

MRS JACKSON: Major Brookes? Have I come to the right room? Mrs Jackson.

MAJOR BROOKES: Mrs Jackson. Yes, of course, I have been expecting you. Come in. I do apologise for the smell. The sewers have backed up again. Did you have difficulty getting here?

MRS JACKSON: There was a bus from Pickering to Whitby. They got one of the old buses working and found some petrol. I came last night and slept in Whitby - with a friend. Then I walked here.

MAJOR BROOKES: All this way. You must be exhausted. I don't know why they put us out here in the middle of nowhere. Out of site, out of mind I expect. How are you getting back?

MRS JACKSON: The bus is leaving again at five. What time is it now?

MAJOR BROOKES: There, look, you can see the clock tower at the end of the barracks. Quarter past two. It's one of the old wind up types so we could keep it going. One of the guards has to get up at five every morning to wind it up and then again in the evening but it's important for us to know the time.

MRS JACKSON: Yes.

MAJOR BROOKES: No, I wont keep you long. Plenty of time to catch the bus. Do excuse me. Let me take your coat. Is that Chloe perfume? I haven't smelled that in a long time. My wife used to ... Where did you get it?

MRS JACKSON: We found a bottle at my Grandmother's house when we had to clear it. I think we gave it her for Christmas ten years ago.

MAJOR BROOKES: I see. Please sit down. Would you like a drink of water, we can just about manage that?

MRS JACKSON: Thank you. What is this about? Why have you called me in?

MAJOR BROOKES: Just a few quick questions. I wont keep you long and then you can be back on your way.

MRS JACKSON: I can't think why you would be interested in me.

MAJOR BROOKES: No, not you really but your brother.

MRS JACKSON: My brother?

MAJOR BROOKES: Yes but a few preliminaries first. I need to fill in this form. Make sure I am talking to the right person at least.

MRS JACKSON: Yes.

MAJOR BROOKES: Name, Mrs ... your first name?

MRS JACKSON: Freya.

MAJOR BROOKES: There's a name you don't hear very often. It was very popular back in the twenties wasn't it? I had a niece called Freya.

MRS JACKSON: Really.

MAJOR BROOKES: So, Mrs Freya Jackson, 27 Morlands Road, Pickering, Northumbria. Not Yorkshire as some people insist on writing on their forms. Until we put them right. Northumbria. Widow?

MRS JACKSON: Yes, my husband was killed in the war - conflict -

MAJOR BROOKES: Misunderstanding ...

MRS JACKSON: Misunderstanding with Mercia.

MAJOR BROOKES: I'm sorry. *(Checking the back of the file)* I see he volunteered. You must be very proud.

MRS JACKSON: No, not proud. We disagreed wholeheartedly about this war. We even argued on the day he left. I wish we hadn't.

MAJOR BROOKES: How did that come to happen? A war with the Scots or Irish or even the French at a push, everyone could understand and support that but the Mercians? Almost like fighting your own kind.

MRS JACKSON: It seems a shame. We know so many people across the Humber. Decent people.

MAJOR BROOKES: A shame. Yes indeed a shame but necessary. If we had lost the South Coal fields then there would have been serious shortages of energy. Wind and solar can only do so much. You must miss your husband?

MRS JACKSON: I think about him every day. I miss the companionship and the talk; he was a sceptic on all matters religious and political and the sex, oh how I miss the sex. I am sorry that was inappropriate for this situation.

MAJOR BROOKES: Not at all. You are very honest. So you brother is all that you have?

MRS JACKSON: No, there is a sister but about my brother ...

MAJOR BROOKES: Just a moment, nearly there. Your brother has no family?

MRS JACKSON: No, he never seemed to meet the right girl.

MAJOR BROOKES: You have your widow's war pension and you work?

MRS JACKSON: Yes, I get some hours at the military hospital in ophthalmology ... I help the blind.

MAJOR BROOKES: Is it true that your other senses compensate?

MRS JACKSON: Absolutely, that's why people with no sense of humour have an increased sense of self importance.

MAJOR BROOKES: So you get by. It would be a shame, hard for you, if you were to lose your job and pension. How would you manage?

MRS JACKSON: Is there a problem? I ...

MAJOR BROOKES: No, no, of course not. I am just being hypothetical. But I am sure you are aware that anyone with a criminal record cannot be employed by the state and has no pension entitlements. Still, that wont apply to you will it? There is no need to go down that road is there? I am sure you will cooperate fully. Did you remember to bring your passport, for identification?

MRS JACKSON: Yes, here.

MAJOR BROOKES: Thank you. I'll have to hold on to it for a while; - until the electricity is back and the copier is working. I need to take a copy. You weren't thinking of going anywhere were you?

MRS JACKSON: No, of course not. Where would I go?

MAJOR BROOKES: New Zealand perhaps? Your sister in New Zealand?

105

MRS JACKSON: Sally. I haven't heard from her in such a long time.

MAJOR BROOKES: Not a card or a letter?

MRS JACKSON: No nothing and since the web got restricted I haven't heard from her. I worried at first but then the mail and the phone system ... well you know. I suppose she has her own life to live but it would be nice to hear, just to know they are all right.

MAJOR BROOKES: Family can be so thoughtless.

MRS JACKSON: Yes. Do you have any family?

MAJOR BROOKES: No.

MRS JACKSON: You mentioned a niece ...

MAJOR BROOKES: So what do you do in your spare time, when you are not working or worrying about your family?

MRS JACKSON: Yes, my brother, you said you were interested in my brother.

MAJOR BROOKES: Any hobbies or pastimes?

MRS JACKSON: I sing with the local Musical Society; musicals. Gilbert and Sullivan, that sort of thing. I don't have much of a voice so I stand at the back of the chorus.

MAJOR BROOKES: To add some glamour.

MRS JACKSON: To make up the numbers. It gets me out of the house and a chance to meet people.

MAJOR BROOKES: What are you doing now?

MRS JACKSON: *The Mikado*. Do you know it?

MAJOR BROOKES: Oh yes. What's that lovely tune at the beginning of the second act? 'The sun whose rays ... tum tum te tum ...'

MRS JACKSON: *(sings)*
The sun, whose rays
Are all ablaze

With ever-living glory,
Does not deny
His majesty
He scorns to tell a story!

Well, you can see why I am in the chorus.

MAJOR BROOKES: Not at all. Lovely. Good old Gilbert and Sullivan eh? They've gone a bit out of fashion now but I don't think you can beat them for all-round entertainment. We did them at school. A bit bizarre really as we were all boys. The young boys had to play the women's parts and wear padded bras to make the costumes fit. I played 'The Lord High Executioner' when we did *The Mikado. (he sings)* 'I've got a little list, I've got a little list, And I don't think they'll be missed, I'm sure they wont be missed.' Would you be missed Freya? May I call you Freya?

MRS JACKSON: Yes, yes of course. How do you mean?

MAJOR BROOKES: You know, if you didn't turn up for work or rehearsal, would you be missed, would people worry, call at the house to see if you were all right? Your friend in Whitby - I didn't catch her name.

MRS JACKSON: I like to think so.

MAJOR BROOKES: Name?

MRS JACKSON: Sarah Ellis.

MAJOR BROOKES: But you couldn't be sure.

MRS JACKSON: No, I suppose not. Who could be?

MAJOR BROOKES: Indeed. Except in the armed services, of course. They keep a close eye on us here. Everyone checks on everyone else to see we are where we should be, doing what we should be doing.

MRS JACKSON: Must seem claustrophobic. What were you before the wars, misunderstandings, began?

MAJOR BROOKES: A teacher.

MRS JACKSON: Really? What did you teach?

107

MAJOR BROOKES: History.

MRS JACKSON: I loved history but then I suppose I was in love with the history teacher. School girl crush and all that.

MAJOR BROOKES: I hope he didn't take advantage of you. Did he?

MRS JACKSON: Mr Simmons. Good Lord, no. I doubt he knew I even existed. Sat at the back of the class, nose in my book, just glimpsing up at him now and again.

MAJOR BROOKES: No inappropriate conversations, touching, that sort of thing?

MRS JACKSON: No. No, nothing like that at all.

MAJOR BROOKES: Good. Now, about your brother.

MRS JACKSON: Yes.

MAJOR BROOKES: Has he been in touch. A phone call perhaps?

MRS JACKSON: No, no phone calls.

MAJOR BROOKES: Of course not, we would know. A letter, a card?

MRS JACKSON: Wouldn't you know about those as well?

MAJOR BROOKES: Yes, we would but people are clever, cunning. They can leave letters in secret places, where they are picked up when no one knows. We can't follow everyone all the time. Do you have a secret place where your brother leaves letters, Mrs Jackson?

MRS JACKSON: No, nothing. I haven't heard from John since, since he went missing. Why are you so interested in him?

MAJOR BROOKES: You can't pretend you don't know. Come along Mrs Jackson, Freya.

MRS JACKSON: Really, no. When Johnny went missing, I reported it to the police and they came round and took a statement. . .

MAJOR BROOKES: This statement? *(He hands her a sheet of paper from his file)*

MRS JACKSON: Yes. They said they would be in touch if they heard anything but there has been nothing. And I haven't heard anything. Why are you so interested in him? He's just a boy.

MAJOR BROOKES: We are interested in everyone who goes missing. You do want him found don't you?

MRS JACKSON: Yes, of course but if this is a missing persons enquiry then surely the police ...

MAJOR BROOKES: There are certain people who we take a particular interest in, so we assist the police in their enquiries. We are very interested in your brother.

MRS JACKSON: Why?

MAJOR BROOKES: Let us just say that he has associated with people the Government consider dangerous, likely to cause unrest and dissent at the very time when unity and calm are needed.

MRS JACKSON: Who? What sort of people?

MAJOR BROOKES: We were hoping you could help us there. Give us the names of people you know your brother was friendly with or was associated with in any way.

MRS JACKSON: Who?

MAJOR BROOKES: Well, lets begin with the people he went to school with. Is he still in touch with any of them?

MRS JACKSON: I really couldn't be sure. I know he goes out for a drink with some old friends when he is home but who they are, their names, I am not sure of.

MAJOR BROOKES: Come along now, Freya. That wont do. I find it difficult to believe that you can't give me the names of the young men John was friendly with all through his teens and early twenties. They must have visited your house on numerous occasions. Are you telling me a young woman like you took no notice of your brother's friends?

109

MRS JACKSON: Well, yes, yes, I suppose I did.

MAJOR BROOKES: Then their names please? We need to eliminate them from our enquiries. After all, if John has gone into hiding somewhere, his old school friends are as likely as anyone to give him shelter. All we would do is visit their homes, do a quick check and if he isn't there, then no more would be said.

MRS JACKSON: But I am still not sure what you want him for? What has he done to make you interested in him?

MAJOR BROOKES: That really is no concern of yours. As a citizen of Northumbria it is you duty to assist the authorities in every way, if they ask for your help. Look, if you don't want to tell me, just write the names down. *(He pushes a piece of paper and a pen towards her)* Just two names will do. They will lead to the rest.

MRS JACKSON: I can't.

MAJOR BROOKES: Why not?

MRS JACKSON: It wouldn't be right.

MAJOR BROOKES: What? It wouldn't be right to help the authorities who are trying to protect you, to defend you? At the very time when opposing armies are not fifty miles from where we are sitting. It wouldn't be right to write down just one name and then you would be able to walk free from here, I promise you, and get on with your life. Your job and pension would be secure. If your brother is innocent, then he has nothing to fear and neither have you! What is 'not right' about that?

MRS JACKSON: I just feel it wouldn't be right. He is my brother.

MAJOR BROOKES: And there we have it. There we have why we have to track down your brother and everyone like him. Everyone like you.

MRS JACKSON: I don't understand.

MAJOR BROOKES: You are people of faith. You 'just feel'. You cannot be reasoned with. You have beliefs. You take for true what cannot be proved. You are a danger to yourselves and our whole community.

MRS JACKSON: I am not clear ...

MAJOR BROOKES: Look, I can tell you that cows have four legs and you can tell me that you believe they have three. I can take you to any dairy farm of your choice and we can count the legs. We can call up pictures on the internet, read veterinary reports, have independent people of your own choice go out and find cows and count their legs and they would all say that cows have four legs, the proof is undeniable. And yet you would tell me that you still believe that cows have three legs.

MRS JACKSON: Cows ...?

MAJOR BROOKES: The same with religion. Since Darwin and the great philosophers and our own empirical experience, the proof is overwhelming that there is no God. And yet you sit there and tell me there is. How can you prove it? You don't have to prove it because belief in an unseen deity is not capable of rational proof, is beyond the limited understanding of man. It is a matter of faith. We must all take the leap of faith required to come to an understanding of the All Mighty.

MRS JACKSON: You have no religion in your life, Major Brookes?

MAJOR BROOKES: Do I look like a fool Mrs Jackson? Do I?

MRS JACKSON: No, of course not.

MAJOR BROOKES: Then why expect me to behave like one? Yes, of course I started out like everyone else believing in God. I went to school, put my hands together and closed my eyes. 'Our father who art in heaven ...' Because I was born in this country it was the Christian God but if chance had had me born in India I would have been praying to Buddhist Gods and if in Africa to Allah. If things went well then God was pleased, if they went badly then it must have been something we had done to annoy him. But it didn't take long for anyone with half a brain to see through all that and reason it out for myself.

MRS JACKSON: Surely having faith, believing in something beyond ourselves is not foolish? So many people down the ages have found comfort, a meaning to their lives and deaths in what you call foolish.

MAJOR BROOKES: 'God is in his heaven, All is right with the world.'

MRS JACKSON: Of course, I'm no theologian but hasn't the idea of an old man on a cloud looking down on us and rewarding the good and punishing the bad rather had its day?

MAJOR BROOKES: You would be surprised. I discount children and the feeble minded of course, but you would be surprised how many people I have in here who sit in that chair and tell me that God is watching everything I do and say and that I should repent and bow down before him before it is too late and I go straight to hell.

MRS JACKSON: And what do you say to them?

MAJOR BROOKES: What can I say? They are not open to discussion and argument or reason. They are right because they have faith and I am wrong because I haven't. And so we - deal with them.

MRS JACKSON: 'Deal with them' - what does that mean?

MAJOR BROOKES: That really is no concern of yours. Not yet. We are a long way from that point in our discussions.

MRS JACKSON: But I am still not clear, I don't understand what all this has to do with John? What has he actually done that you should take all this trouble over him?

MAJOR BROOKES: Done? Well, he hasn't done anything - not yet. But that is why this department was set up. To track down and find those people who most likely will do something; something which will do harm to the people of Northumbria. If we can stop these despised people before they act, then a great deal of damage and distress will be stopped before it is done. But let's not get caught up in all the niceties of religion shall we? Whether the host is present or it isn't, whether priests should grow beards or be clean-shaven, celibate or married, whether we worship in silence or sing hymns or any of the other trivia the religions of this world have thought it worth dying and killing for.

MRS JACKSON: But that is all behind us now. You must admit that the churches do a lot of good. We run charities, look after the sick and the dying and orphan children.

MAJOR BROOKES: Not the children. We stopped that.

MRS JACKSON: Yes, oh yes, I was forgetting.

MAJOR BROOKES: 'Keep a child away from religion until he is seven and he has every chance of growing up into a balanced human being, capable of making rational decisions.' That is what the leader said and how right he was.

112

MRS JACKSON: You know I was against that and the closing of the faith schools. I suppose all that is in your file.

MAJOR BROOKES: Oh yes. Your speech to the national assembly and the newspaper articles, radio, television. The big demonstration that brought Sheffield to a standstill. You became quite a national figure - still are I suppose.

MRS JACKSON: It was something I believed in.

MAJOR BROOKES: What was it exactly you believed in?

MRS JACKSON: That parents should have the right to choose a faith school for their children, whatever their faith.

MAJOR BROOKES: Of course, now I remember. The State had to oppose you, of course. Bringing innocent children up in an environment slanted to one particular ideology at such a tender age, caused irreparable damage; almost a kind of child abuse.

MRS JACKSON: Surely not ...

MAJOR JACKSON: Not to mention the social divisions it caused. Catholics fighting Protestants again in Northern Ireland, Christians against Muslims in Bradford, Muslims against Sikhs in Birmingham. How many died in the last riots, did they ever come to a firm figure?

MRS JACKSON: Those riots cannot be put down solely to religious differences. There were so many other factors involved, poverty, housing, jobs.

MAJOR BROOKES: But all gathered together under the religious umbrella because that is what all those children, those young people, educated in their segregated schools   felt they had in common. Us against them. Us against the Catholics with their foreign imposed views and us against the Muslims with their funny habits and funny ways, taking our jobs and abusing our women while their women were never allowed to leave the house, let alone work and choose their own husbands because that is what their religion demanded.

MRS JACKSON: So many religious leaders were down on the streets, pleading for calm and tolerance. You can't accuse us all of bigotry.

MAJOR JACKSON: No, not all but enough of you. Enough to put the very existence of the State in jeopardy. You can understand why we had to make a stand and abolishing the faith schools was a logical start. But you have moved on since then.

MRS JACKSON: How?

MAJOR JACKSON: What is it now? Opposition to the war. Look for a peaceful way. End the killing and so on and so on.

MRS JACKSON: Everybody wants the war to end, the pointless killing and suffering. Surely if we can find a way to come to some sort of agreement then it has to be preferable.

MAJOR JACKSON: Indeed. Everyone wants to get back to normal and the leader is meeting his counterpart this weekend at a neutral, secret location. Yes, I am telling you that Mrs Freya Jackson. But you and your like with all this talk of surrender and passive resistance have left him weak and at a disadvantage. But we are straying away from your brother. We really need to speak to him. Before it is too late.

MRS JACKSON: Too late? Too late for what?

MAJOR BROOKES: A keen gardener is he, your brother?

MRS JACKSON: Good Lord, no. He wouldn't know a weed from an orchid.

MAJOR BROOKES: Then how do you explain this? *(He passes her a sheet of paper)*

MRS JACKSON: What is it?

MAJOR BROOKES: A copy of your brother's credit card statement. You will notice item five. 'Six bags of chemical fertilizer'. If he's not a gardener or smallholder, why would he want those?

MRS JACKSON: I really couldn't say.

MAJOR BROOKES: Couldn't you? You know that nitrate based fertilizer, such as the ones your brother has bought in such large quantities is the primary ingredient in a home made explosive device - a bomb? Perhaps you can see now, begin to understand just why we are so interested in seeing your brother before he has time to act?

114

MRS JACKSON: I am sure there is a perfectly logical explanation ...

MAJOR BROOKES: Really? I look forward to hearing it. Well?

MRS JACKSON: This is just circumstantial evidence. No, you must be mistaken. John had never harmed anyone in his life. He wouldn't, he couldn't.

MAJOR BROOKES: And how many times have I heard that? "Michael is such a good boy. He would never hurt anyone. What? He has assassinated a Government minister? No, that can't be right! He goes to church. He has never been in trouble in his life." Oh yes, Mrs Jones, your dear Michael got it into his head that our devoted Minister for Defence was the cause of all the country's troubles so he got hold of a gun - and we would like to know from where - stepped out of the crowd and blew Mr Clements' brains out. And then shot himself before the guards could get hold of him. He did manage to shout, 'God is great' before shooting himself, which I suppose makes a change from the 'Allahu Akbah' from earlier in the century. You remember when those nice young boys from Leeds went to London and killed 52 innocent   people and maimed seven hundred more on the underground and buses, and blew themselves to Paradise where they were ministered to by a dozen or is it twenty virgins, I can never remember? Anyway the result is the same. Good people die because people of faith think they have the right to take life to foster their irrational beliefs. John fits the profile perfectly. We have to find him before he does harm to himself and who knows how many others.

MRS JACKSON: I really think you must be mistaken. You don't know John or you wouldn't say such things.

MAJOR BROOKES: Your judgement is clouded by family love and sentiment. If you could look at the facts logically and rationally, you would come to a different conclusion and be willing to help us find your brother.

MRS JACKSON: You say 'he fits the profile'. What do you mean?

MAJOR BROOKES: Over the last few years since religious and political fanatics - and the two often go hand in hand - have been killing in the name of whatever God or country they believe in, we have been looking at their lives and their beliefs and a clear pattern emerges. If we can fit the person to the pattern and eliminate him, before harm is done, then we can do a lot of good. Believe me your brother fits the pattern.

MRS JACKSON: Does he?

MAJOR BROOKES: Oh yes. Below average intelligence. Somewhat alienated from society because of a lack of job opportunities. A lack of self-esteem because of early failures in life. No serious love life - they usually find it difficult to relate to the opposite sex. Possessor of terrorist skills - he loves radios doesn't he? - so a prime target for recruitment and, of course, member of a religious group prone to demonstrate and be awkward and to clash with the police. So resentment builds up and the habit of protest begins early. Peaceful at first then more aggressive then downright violent and deadly. Does this all sound familiar? Isn't this your beloved John?

MRS JACKSON: If, if I helped you find him. What would happen to him?

MAJOR BROOKES: If we could get to him before he did any harm then the charge would be planning terrorism. If he helped us trace his accomplices then there would be a prison sentence, not too long, he would still be a young man when he got out. But if we are too late, then there is only the firing squad. And the death of who knows how many innocent citizens. But we are prejudging. There would be an investigation, a trial. He may well be innocent as you say. But are you willing to take that chance Mrs Jackson?

MRS JACKSON: No. No I can see that ... but it is so difficult.

MAJOR BROOKES: I understand We all love our families.

MRS JACKSON: Would I be able to see him?

MAJOR BROOKES: I can't promise but I will do everything I can to give you some time together.

MRS JACKSON: Thank you. He is staying with my friend in Whitby.

MAJOR BROOKES: Sarah Ellis?

MRS JACKSON: Yes.

MAJOR BROOKES: Address?

MRS JACKSON: 14 The Rise.

MAJOR BROOKES: Thank you. Excuse me. *(He phones)* Sergeant Scott. Major Brookes. Jackson is at 14 The Rise in Whitby. Send a squad and pick him up and go easy on him. Yes. Yes.

116

MRS JACKSON: *(Crying)* I felt there was something wrong the moment he went missing, without saying a word.

MAJOR BROOKES: It must have been difficult for you betraying your brother like that but now it is done and we can move on. To you.

MRS JACKSON: Me? I ...

MAJOR BROOKES: Now that you have shown you are willing to help the authorities and your role in your brother's arrest is bound to come out at his trial, then the next thing we want from you will not be so difficult.

MRS JACKSON: What is it? What do you want now? Surely I have done enough?

MAJOR BROOKES: All we want is for you to sign this simple statement which we would release to the media and then read it out and answer a few questions - for which we would provide the answers - on the main news tonight. This evening, before the leader's meeting this weekend.

MRS JACKSON: What does the statement say? What would I have to say? Why me?

MAJOR BROOKES: Because, Mrs Jackson, you are known. People know your face, you are a celebrity in your own small way. A statement from you would carry much more weight than a dozen appeals from Ministers of State or military leaders. Even the leader himself. People trust you. You are known for your sincerity and independence of mind.

MRS JACKSON: What does it say, this statement?

MAJOR BROOKES: Here, read it yourself. It is short but to the point.

MRS JACKSON: *(reads)* 'In our time of national crisis, when the whole nation must pull together, I realise my opposition to the Government's policies and war effort have been sadly mistaken and counter-productive.   I call upon all my supporters and people of faith to remain calm, stop their opposition activities and get behind our leader in his attempts to secure our future in peace and security. I renounce my faith in God and put my faith into the hands of our leader who will surely see us through.' This is ridiculous. No one will believe I wrote this.

MAJOR BROOKES: Well, now you read it out it does sound rather simplistic but you are free to adapt it to make it sound more like your own words, as long as the message stays the same.

MRS JACKSON: You ask too much.

MAJOR BROOKES: I ask nothing. If it was down to me you could walk out that door now. But this request comes from the very top and I have strict orders not to let you go until you sign that paper and agree to make the broadcast.

MRS JACKSON: And what will happen to you if I refuse to sign?

MAJOR BROOKES: That is my concern. If I were you, I would be more worried about myself.

MRS JACKSON: Is that a threat?

MAJOR BROOKES: *(Draws his pistol)* If I were to put this to your head and begin to squeeze the trigger, that would be a threat. But don't be afraid, it is perfectly safe. You have never been this close to a weapon before have you? Here take it. Take it. Look, it is really very simple. You release the safety catch here. Cock it so and then aim and squeeze the trigger Bang. Here take it, try it.

MRS JACKSON: No, I couldn't. I never ...

MAJOR BROOKES: Take it! *(Mrs Jackson takes the pistol, releases the safety catch and cocks the pistol. Major Jackson, grabs her hand and forces the pistol to his forehead).* Go on, pull the trigger, pull it! You would be doing me a huge favour.

MRS JACKSON: *(She screams and lets go of the pistol, leaving it in Major Brookes hands. He slowly puts the pistol onto the table).*Please, I ...

MAJOR BROOKES: Yes, yes I know. You are a peaceable person, couldn't hurt anyone, let alone shoot them.

MRS JACKSON: What did you mean, I would be doing you a favour?

MAJOR BROOKES: Nothing. Really nothing.

MRS JACKSON: It was just such a strange thing to say. Are you tired of life? Is it this job? I ...

MAJOR BROOKES: Five years ago I was like you. I had my job. My family. Of course, we were all worried about the wars, who wasn't?

MRS JACKSON: Something happened?

MAJOR BROOKES: We were walking through the streets of York. My wife and daughter and my niece, Freya. Her parents had been killed in a raid. A day out to see the sites. I left them for a moment to look into a shop window. Just a moment. Just around the corner. Antiques. I went in and bought this paperweight for my wife. She collected them, loved them, all over the house. As soon as I heard the explosion, I knew they were gone. They must have been standing right next to him. All we found were parts, all mingled together with the bomber and other people who had been walking past. All buried in a mass grave. And do you know what the bomber said on the video the police got the next day?

MRS JACKSON: No.

MAJOR BROOKES: He had felt a call from God. An inner light had burned in him, directing him to make this protest against the war, against all wars. He had to follow his conscience, to trust in his faith in God. He was sorry if anyone had to die but in the long run, it would be for everyone's benefit. God was his witness and guide.

MRS JACKSON: I see. Then this job ...

MAJOR BROOKES: I volunteered soon afterwards. I had done my service years ago but they were short of men and despite my age they gave me my old rank back and posted me here. Cathartic, they thought. A chance to track down other people like that bomber and make sure it didn't happen to another family.

MRS JACKSON: Look, this statement. I could agree to the first part of it, adapted slightly perhaps. Now that I know the leader is trying to talk, to bring an end to the war, then I should get behind him. I could say, 'In our time of national crisis, when the whole nation *should* pull together, I realise my opposition to the Government's policies and war effort have been *temporarily misplaced* and counter-productive. I call upon all my supporters and people of faith to remain calm, stop their *current* opposition activities and get behind our leader in his attempts to secure our future in peace and security.' Wouldn't that do?

MAJOR BROOKES: It might well be all right. I would need to get it cleared but it sounds reasonable, more like you in fact.

MRS JACKSON: Good.

MAJOR BROOKES: But the second part, 'I renounce my faith in God and put my faith into the hands of our leader who will surely see us through.' You don't mention that.

MRS JACKSON: Surely that can't be necessary. The state has always upheld freedom of religious worship.

MAJOR BROOKES: You are right of course. We have always followed a policy of not interfering in matters which are no concern of the state. What goes on behind closed doors between consenting adults is a matter for them, not us. Whether you are a homosexual or a stamp collector or a Christian, we really don't care as long as you go on paying your taxes and stay behind those closed doors. But, of course, you wont, will you. Oh you pay your taxes rightly enough, even though some of you make noises about the morality of this war and stand around with your banners but we ignore that, turn a blind eye. We know you will go home to your tea and television once you have made your statement. Very few of you have the conviction strong enough to go into politics and try and make things change from the inside. So I suppose we have to be grateful for that at least. But you, you are different. You actually seem to believe what you say and are prepared to get into the political arena and mix it with the big boys and that is why they don't care for you. Maybe they are a little afraid of you. So this statement will serve two purposes.

MRS JACKSON: Which are?

MAJOR BROOKES: Firstly, discredit you politically. All those things you have been saying about peace and passive resistance turned out to be wrong didn't they? You were wrong in the past, so why should anyone believe anything you say in the future. You would be finished, politically speaking. The many people who follow you will fall in line and the position of our leader will be strengthened.

MRS JACKSON: And secondly? My renunciation in my belief in God. How ridiculous. No one will believe that for a moment. Why do you even demand it of me?

MAJOR BROOKES: No, its not very well expressed but civil servants with theology degrees are hard to come by nowadays. But the thought behind it is really quite subtle. It's true we are on new ground here, demanding that our citizens take an oath of allegiance to the leader and renouncing their religious beliefs but you can see the point.

MRS JACKSON: No, I can't. Not at all.

MAJOR BROOKES: I suppose it is history going into reverse. We used to demand that citizens *did* take an oath that they believed in God and all his ways and those who refused were burned at the stake, branded, had their tongues bored through or at the least banished from the country. Religion and the state were one

120

and the same. It still goes on of course. Blaspheme against Allah or the Koran and the civil authorities step in and off to prison or the executioner you go.

MRS JACKSON: But not in this country.

MAJOR BROOKES: No. Not for a long time. We managed to separate Church and State - the good old Church of England hardly counts. They quickly fell into line. It's easy with any hierarchy. Persuade the top man and most of the rest follow on blindly enough. Those who put up a resistance are reminded of their duties to tend their flocks and their free houses and pensions and the safety of their families and they see the sense of the proposals and sign the paper.

MRS JACKSON: That's what you did to me, isn't it? And those who wont fall into line and sign?

MAJOR BROOKES: Oh they all do in the end. As will you.

MRS JACKSON: No, because my eternal soul is of far greater importance to me . I'm not going to sign the paper. No matter what you do to me I am not going to renounce my faith in God. He is my Creator, my Father. The Lord Jesus didn't die on the cross and rise again for nothing. He died because he loves us so much. He died so our sins can be forgiven, we can have a relationship with the Father, we can have eternal life with him. I have an inheritance in heaven that will never perish, spoil or fade   and you can have that too if you just believe, repent and follow him. God is loving, God is good, he cannot lead us into evil ways, it's our sinful nature that does that. God gives us a choice how to live, to follow him which leads to life or ourselves which leads to death.

MAJOR BROOKES: God is what you make him and the excuse of using his name has let evil people do evil things for centuries. It has to stop or no-one is safe from the fanatic, the zealot, the rifleman, the suicide bomber.

MRS JACKSON: You take the extreme case all the time. Most people of faith are good people, caring people who could no more do the evil things you mention than a child. People who commit evil in the name of God are troubled people, people who need help, not condemnation.

MAJOR BROOKES: And who is to decide who is troubled and who is the prophet? Wasn't your man Jesus seen as a trouble maker and put to death by the authorities? What should they have done? Let him lead his little revolt and plunge the region into chaos?

121

MRS JACKSON: Our Lord Jesus was a man of peace. His kingdom was not of this earth.

MAJOR BROOKES: It certainly wasn't once they had smashed his hand against the cross. We digress. Look, just sign the paper. Most people have, you know. You don't have to believe it. Just sign, make your broadcast and once the peace treaty is signed we will leave you alone, let you get back to your old ways. The pressure will be off. People will understand.

MRS JACKSON: I cannot. I could not live with myself. Just let me go and I will keep quiet for the next week. I wont cause any problems for you.

MAJOR BROOKES: I can't let you go. You can see that. I have my orders. You will need to stay here for the next few days until the political situation is clearer. I am sure the guards will look after you. They don't get much female company out here. You wont mind sharing their quarters will you, we are so short of guest accommodation?

MRS JACKSON: No, you cannot. For pity's sake I ...

MAJOR BROOKES: Just sign the paper and I will take you back to Whitby myself, now. With your brother. I am authorised to release him if you will cooperate.

MRS JACKSON: And how long will it be before we are picked up again, brought back here?

MAJOR BROOKES: You have my word. Leave the country if you like. Here is your passport. *(He throws her her passport)*

MRS JACKSON: Where would I go?

MAJOR BROOKES: Wherever you like. We would provide the flight for both of you. New Zealand. Your sister is anxious to hear from you, to see you again.

MRS JACKSON: What?

MAJOR BROOKES: Here, read for yourself. *(He throws her a bundle of letters).* They seem to have been held up in the post.

MRS JACKSON: *(Looking through the bundle)* How long?

MAJOR BROOKES: Look at the dates. Work it out yourself. She and her husband are doing very well. They have a daughter you know. Plenty of room for you and John.

MRS JACKSON: You have read them?

MAJOR BROOKES: Yes. It's my job. Sign the paper, make the broadcast and all your troubles are over.

MRS JACKSON: Give me some time.

MAJOR BROOKES: Time is what we are short of. Either sign the paper or I pick up the phone and hand you over to Sergeant Scott and I doubt that you and your brother will be heard about for a long time. *(He sings)* 'And if you remain callous and obdurate, You will perish as he did and you will know why, Though you probably will not exclaim as you die, Oh willow, tit willow, tit willow ...'

MRS JACKSON: Stop it! Stop it! No, I cannot, will not!

MAJOR BROOKES: 'Oh Willow, tit willow, tit willow ...'

MRS JACKSON: Stop!

(He grabs her left hand and smashes the paperweight down onto her hand. She lets out a piercing cry and collapses onto the desk
)
MAJOR BROOKES: That was your little finger. Your ring finger is next. *(He raises the weight).*

MRS JACKSON: No, please, no.

MAJOR BROOKES: Sign the paper!

MRS JACKSON: Please, no. *(He brings down the paperweight again).*

MAJOR BROOKES: That was your ring finger. Your middle finger is next. Sign the paper! *(He raises the weight).*

MRS JACKSON: All right, please don't hurt me anymore. *(She signs).*

MAJOR BROOKES: There now, that wasn't so difficult was it. Why you couldn't have done that right from the beginning so that all this unpleasantness could have been avoided, I cannot understand. *(He phones)* Hello, Major Brookes. Send a medic to ... What? I'll come at once. *(He leaves)*.

(Mrs Jackson sits crying, rocking herself. She sees Major Brooke's pistol which he has left on the desk. She picks it up, releases the safety catch and puts the gun to her head. Major Brookes enters.)

Don't do that. It would be rather ironic if you did. *(Mrs Jackson points the gun at Major Brookes)* And I have told you already, death would come as a welcome release. Not that you could anyway. *(He begins to quickly pack his briefcase with papers and personal effects. Mrs Jackson puts the gun back on the desk)*

MRS JACKSON: What is going on? What is happening?

MAJOR BROOKES: There has been a break through. Mercian forces are in Scarborough and heading this way. The talk of peace was just a ruse, a cover to put us off our guard over this offensive. We are ordered to withdraw to Newcastle.

MRS JACKSON: And me?

MAJOR BROOKES: I have no idea. Pray to your God and see if he comes up with a solution.

MRS JACKSON: My brother?

MAJOR BROOKES: Safe in Whitby; my men never made it through. He will be quite a hero once the Mercians take over. I suppose as the hero's sister you will be safe enough. Just hang on here and you will be found. Here, keep you case papers and what with your injuries, you will be believed.

MRS JACKSON: And you?

MAJOR BROOKES: I neither know nor care. I follow orders and head for Newcastle. If I live, I live, if I die I die.

MRS JACKSON: Does life mean so little to you?

MAJOR BROOKES: What have I to live for? Family? None. Job and career? None. A faith to live by? None. A woman to love? Nobody.

MRS JACKSON: Take me with you. Your prisoner.

MAJOR BROOKES: After all that has taken place in this room? You want to come with me, probably to certain death if we are caught?

MRS JACKSON: Yes.

MAJOR BROOKES: Then you are madder than I thought you were.

MRS JACKSON: Not mad. Irrational maybe and driven by my heart rather than my head, I admit. But I know that love is greater than hate and that behind that austere face and demeanour is a loving man who has been twisted by hate and the longing for revenge and only needs to follow the light.

MAJOR BROOKES: Mad as a hatter. Very well, if you wont stay here, there is room in the Land Rover, as my prisoner, if we are captured.

MRS JACKSON: And if we make it through to Newcastle?

MAJOR BROOKES: Sgt Scott will drive you straight to the airport and put you on a plane. You can make your own way after that.

MRS JACKSON: You would do that? Why?

MAJOR BROOKES: God knows.

MRS JACKSON: Yes, he does.

MAJOR BROOKES: What? Oh, a slip of the tongue. Old habits from my childhood. Go on, the vehicle is waiting outside. I need to finish off here.

MRS JACKSON: *(Picks up the paperweight)* Aren't you taking this?

MAJOR BROOKES: No, leave it. *(Mrs Jackson puts the weight down on the table).* Too many painful memories. Too many ... Look, I am sorry about what happened here. You have every right to ...

MRS JACKSON: I think I can understand. I can certainly forgive.

MAJOR BROOKES: Very Christian of you.

MRS JACKSON: Yes. We should go.

MAJOR BROOKES: Here, take this. It's a travel warrant. Give it to Sgt Scott and tell him to get you on a military plane to Edinburgh. From there you can make it abroad.

MRS JACKSON: What about you?

MAJOR BROOKES: I am still a serving officer. I will take my chances at Newcastle. The war could soon be over.

MRS JACKSON: Over?

MAJOR BROOKES: (*Lowering his voice*) The war is going very badly. Much worse than is generally known. You should try and get to New Zealand if you can. By boat if you have to.

MRS JACKSON: What will happen to you?

MAJOR BROOKES: Prisoner of war. Back to teaching if I am released. Prison or the firing squad if people like you come forward.

MRS JACKSON: You can't spirit us all away to New Zealand.

MAJOR BROOKES: That's right. There's a medic in the convoy, get him to look at that hand. Now go will you, Sgt Scott wont wait forever. *(She places her hand on his shoulder. Exit Mrs Jackson. Major Brookes sits at his desk, tearing papers. He toys with the paper weight. Picks up the pistol, cocks it. Lights fade. Music.)*

END